The Inspector remained ~~~~~~~~~~~~~~~~~~~~~~
wounds. Certainly they we~~~~~~~~~~~~~~~~~~~~~~
but they could have been m~~~~~~~~~~~~~~~~~~~mine, or
spike, and a rhythmic swing, running out of energy or sadistic
inclination. Sergeant, I want you to find that missing Filipino
— and fast.''

Wadkin made off into the twilight. Before re-entering
Mitchell Hall, Bantree paused to wonder why anyone killed by
a fall should then be mutilated, transported twenty miles,
deposited inside a cabin cruiser, and set alight.
''Camouflage,'', he said he himself. ''The real question is did
he fall or was he pushed?''

But Treasure knew that that wasn't really the question at all.

Unholy Writ

David Williams

First Mysterious Press Edition April, 1984

2 4 6 8 0 9 7 5 3 1

Library of Congress Catalogue Card Number: 83-63284
   ISBN: 0-89296-089-2
Published by The Mysterious Press
            129 West 56th Street
            New York, NY 10019

Cover design by Denise Schultheis at the Angelica
   Design Group Ltd.
Cover illustration by John Jinks

Printed in the United States of America

For my Wife
Brenda

THE LETTER

October the Nineteenth, 1644

My dearest and beloved wife,

I praye by all things Sacred that you and our sonne, my pretious heir, shall be safe out of this cursed Island before this word can reach you. If some delay hath prevented you this farre, make haste my love else we are all doomed. Take counsel from youre wise Father on the best course to the coast. If Norfolk is barred – and my Intelligences are so oertaken by events I now am no judge – but if 'tis barred then the man Rorke who bears this note will guide you well to Wales and thence to his native, Catholic Ireland.

This writ, I go to Newbury with the half troupe that remains. There we muster for the King with others survived the dire history of this year. If the Victorie is ours then Fortune could return, but there is little heart and more of Turncoats in the counties here around where once commitment to our cause was greatest. Were we defeated and I spared, then pray for my life and sword for I will fight still while I have breath and there be ten of us to wreake a vengeance on this tyrant Cromwell, Anti-Christ and Heretic.

With life at stake I have no mind for baubles, and 'tis well so. Our Properties here will fall to plunder or to forfeit left unguarded as now they must be. Take note though, should you ever here return in calm and rightful times, I have this day without the knowledge of a living Soul stor'd up in secret safety the jewels you did in haste forget at our sad departing. And with these are such other Valuables as I could with ease transport into the chamber of the tomb – trinkets, some silver, the gold plates, and – for sentiment – the Manuscript of the Will. Shake-Speare Playe in Arden Forest that my dear Father did prize so much, though 'tis of little value. The last survived so long 'tis fitting it be buried in the ground where it began.

The tunnel to the place from the Pavilion cellar is clos'd and blockt by earth and stone made ready for such Work when first the tomb was fashioned. We'll hear no more our Masses, you and I there, nor the good Father Connell need that protection readied for his sunken chapel – he is safely to France these six weeks since.

Kisse our sonne for me a thousand times, and in the relay of those embraces give mind to him who dispatches in his thoughts ten thousand more to you with this poor script. Think well of him that is your Slave, but Servant also to his King, and love us both for it, for else there is no honoure.

Take care I beseech you, and may St Christopher guard you now, and Blessed Mary all the days of youre life.

> *Youre loving husband*
> *James.*

CHAPTER I

'Bloody hell,' said the Vicar, who was not much given to vulgar expletive in private.

The Reverend Timothy James Trapp, late of Keble College, Oxford, two theological colleges (both wiser for the experience), and more church livings than befitted a bachelor in holy orders not yet thirty, normally reserved his less characteristic clerical pronouncements for larger audiences.

Horace Worple, hedger and ditcher by trade, gravedigger by arrangement, did not constitute a large audience even by the standards of church attendance at St John's, Mitchell Stoke. Nor was he even mildly affected by the Vicar's echoing of his own vehement exclamation; simply, he did not hear it. Digging a grave at the side of a country churchyard was a labour that seldom attracted sightseers. A man so employed could thus rely on the modicum of privacy that suited his disposition, licensed his language, and protected his productivity.

'Hell may be hot,' continued the Vicar in tones that implied he was giving the matter earnest thought, 'but I've never considered the possibility of blood. You could be right though, Mr Worple.'

This time communication was established, with Worple conscious as he straightened his back that a pair of rubber boots overhung by a cassock hem were firmly implanted a few feet above eye-level from where he was standing at the bottom of a very deep hole. Words, too, he realized, were emanating from the six feet of clergyman towering above him.

'Yes, warm for April, Vicar,' he offered, wondering to himself what blood had to do with the weather. Perhaps Trapp had said flood; well, he might be ready with his sea-boots, but the weather forecast had said dry. 'There's rock 'ere,' he went on, 'just 'it it with this pick; given me a nasty jar up both arms.'

'Rock, Mr Worple? Very unusual in this part of the world,' said the Vicar, whose knowledge of geology in Oxfordshire, or for that matter anywhere else, extended to all of one spit. He recalled, though, the diocesan architect observing that the foundations of the west end were sinking into the clay soil.

'Likely or not, I 'it it at seven six.' The Vicar looked at his watch. 'Seven foot six,' continued Worple drily, 'and reckon I'll keep this 'un to the bare seven foot, otherwise 'er'll need a pneumatic. Anyroad, Maggie won't notice no difference.'

Worple was well aware that the customary depth for a single grave was six feet, but since he charged by the foot, he had long established eight feet as a more suitable and seemly measure in a small village cemetery where grave-digging was at best an occasional trade, and competition for the job non-existent. In short, all deceased Anglicans in Mitchell Stoke were afforded 'family depth' repositories whether or not they left any surviving relatives likely to need accommodation at a later date.

The reference to the late departed Miss Margaret Edwards, spinster of the parish for all her seventy-three blameless if wholly uneventful years, set Timothy Trapp thinking in directions entirely unassociated with the curious presence of rock under his own churchyard, not three hundred yards east of the south-flowing Thames, and several miles from known deposits of any substance harder than chalk.

Leaving Worple to contemplate the firm foundation that was to be the Church's final and fitting tribute to the temporal remains of its servant Maggie, the Vicar turned to thread his way eastwards to the gate that led from the churchyard to the broadwalk approach to Mitchell Hall — but not before delivering a friendly kick on the hindquarters of his not altogether faithful retriever Bach, who had employed himself the while doing a little gravedigging on his own account. Instead of immediately falling into step behind his master, Bach treated himself to the luxury of a roll on one of the heaps of subsoil that Worple had arranged with a neatness not improved by the resulting dispersement at one edge. After a generous but indecorous display of his upturned lower stomach and its appurtenances the dog took a friendly sniff at the top of Worple, relieved himself on an adjacent wheelbarrow, and bounded after the Vicar.

Thus it was that Timothy Trapp was the last innocent human to see Worple alive, and Bach the last known recipient of a malevolent glance from that normally mild-mannered son of the soil.

Mitchell Hall, seat of the Moonlight family for seventeen generations, was as well-preserved an example of mid-seventeenth-century country house architecture as you would find in Banister Fletcher or any other book of reference. The fact that it appears neither in the definitive nor the lesser coffee-table works of this nature was in some measure the reason why the thirteenth baronet had so recently, reluctantly, but finally abandoned both residence and ownership.

The Manor of Mitchell Stoke, together with the monastery it contained, had been presented to Sir Francis Moneleet, rogue, fugitive, mercenary, and knight – in that chronological order – by Henry VIII, for services rendered, nominally in defence of the Faith, usefully in the assault of enemy soldiery, secretly in the procurement of pliant females, but privately in the furtherance of personal ambition. The balance of these purposes had been nicely reflected in the actions of Sir Francis, who promptly shot the Abbot, raped his mistress, and looted the monastery, living off the substantial proceeds for the remainder of a fairly dissolute life, even by the standards then applying.

It was not until the reign of James I that a pious Sydney Moonlight attracted sufficient royal favour to be rewarded with a baronetcy. It was his son, tactfully christened James, who succeeded to the title in 1629 and later built himself a mansion that more nearly reflected the family status than the monastic remains that had been adapted for its housing until that period.

It was suggested later that Mitchell Hall had been designed
by Inigo Jones himself. No documentary proof exists to
resolve the matter, but twentieth-century experts have
taken the view that James Moonlight was probably his own
architect, freely adopting ideas from buildings he had seen
in situ or in plan. Although a mannerist composition, the
Hall bears a strong resemblance in one unusual detail to
Stoke Bruerne, a house designed by Jones that existed in
part, and wholly in drawn form, at the time James Moonlight
was a fairly frequent visitor to Northampton. Simply, he
married – and well – into a wealthy Northampton family,
and it is likely that he was taken to see Stoke Bruerne in the
building. It is certain that his wife's substantial dowry
paid for a variation of the same plan – if on a smaller scale –
at Mitchell Stoke.

Executed in flat Palladian style, the house is three storeys
high, including a half basement. On the long, north entrance
frontage the centre three of nine windows are framed from
first-floor level by Ionic half columns. These spring from an
entablature and rise in support of a plain pediment. The
simplicity of this arrangement is somewhat marred by a weak
protruding porch and steps in bad proportion to the rest
of the centre bay.

The southern aspect repeats the pattern of the entrance
front but is more pleasing through the absence of a porch and
basement. Here, on the garden side of the house, long
venetian windows let on to a wide, elevated terrace.

The main pile of the house was originally flanked to the
south by forward-standing, twin-storeyed pavilions linked to
it by curved, enclosed colonnades. It is this feature which is
reminiscent of Stoke Bruerne. Flanking pavilions were
common enough adjuncts to country houses from the
beginning of the eighteenth century, but none such existed
in England – save for the example in Northampton – at the
time Mitchell Hall was building. Indeed, unlike Stoke
Bruerne, which remained uncompleted until after the Civil
War, Mitchell Hall was finished in 1639 when James
Moonlight was reaching the peak of his career and affluence.

A Catholic, James had served the King and the ill-fated Thomas Wentworth, Earl of Strafford. In particular he had helped Strafford in Ireland recruit an army of Catholics destined to put down the rebellious Scots. When Strafford was executed in 1641, James Moonlight repaired to Mitchell Stoke which he made his base, family and military, in good Cavalier country for several years, and well into the period of the Civil War. Being almost mid-way between Oxford and the Marquis of Winchester's Basing House, Mitchell Stoke made an excellent staging post for King's men en route between the two Royalist strongholds. It was however isolated and thus vulnerable to Cromwell's men engaged on eliminating pockets of resistance when the war was drawing to its close in 1645. James himself had perished at the second Battle of Newbury and his home was sacked, then partially destroyed by a company of 'Ironsides'.

The western pavilion was burnt to the ground, but the damage to the rest of the house appears not to have been extensive. The ransacking was uncharacteristic of Cromwell's men, normally well disciplined, and not given to loading themselves down with inedible booty. In this instance the treasures may have proved irresistible -- for treasures there were in plenty.

In the course of his relatively short life, James Moonlight not only built himself a fitting residence, but also filled it with works of art. The quality if not the size of the resulting collection may well have rivalled that inherited and acquired by the third and fourth Earls of Pembroke, two eminent contemporaries, and the brothers to whom Shakespeare's First Folio was dedicated.

Indeed, it is chiefly from family records at their home, Wilton House, and elsewhere, that it is possible to piece together a measure of James's enthusiasm for the arts. He appears to have been a close friend of Philip Herbert, the fourth Earl. Their fathers too had been intimates.

Certainly James stayed at Wilton on at least three occasions, and was a frequent caller at Durham House in the Strand, leased by the Herberts for a number of years. It was

here that Sir Anthony Vandyck painted a full-length portrait
of Sarah Moonlight, James's young wife, shortly after their
marriage in 1638. The quality of the picture is unknown;
it is assumed to have been destroyed in 1645.

James Moonlight made many purchases from the Earl
of Pembroke and others over the years, including paintings,
manuscripts and pieces of sculpture. It is not recorded that
any part of the collection was recovered after the restoration
of the monarchy in 1660. It is known that Sarah Moonlight
returned to Mitchell Hall then, from exile in France, with
her son Francis, the third baronet. Whatever damage was
sustained by the main building was evidently and quickly
restored. This much is on public record since the work was
paid for personally by Charles II, who had established a
special regard for the still young widow while both were in
exile.

The King's attachment to Sarah lasted at least long
enough for the family fortunes to be in part restored along
with the house. Although the western pavilion was not
rebuilt, this may have been a matter of choice and not
necessity. A frail, squat orangery had been constructed over
the site by Commonwealth 'tenants', and Sarah let this
remain, giving then, as now, a somewhat lop-sided appearance to the house on the southern, garden aspect.

The monies that might have been expended in a complete
restoration were perhaps saved for the more practical purpose
of building a modest Dower House some three hundred yards
to the east of Mitchell Hall. This work, commissioned by
Sarah in 1662, is fully documented in records extant at the
Soane Museum. The Third Baronet came of age in that
year. His mother was 39, reason enough for her to be making
provision for her own accommodation in the future – a
future made more bearable by a life pension from King
Charles II – a monarch who recognized an obligation for
services rendered.

The iron gate from the churchyard into the grounds of
Mitchell Hall was locked. What was more, the lock was

new – not that this made a deal of difference to Timothy Trapp since he had never possessed a key for the old lock; in any case he never carried keys. In common with most others who own the same habit, Trapp was quite used to gaining access, when he was entitled, by methods incongruous or even eccentric when compared to the simple process of turning a key. The vicarage was always open, and so was the church; in consequence, both had been promptly relieved of every movable object they had housed worth stealing shortly after Timothy Trapp's installation six months before. From the Vicar's viewpoint the result suited principle and practice. Principle: church buildings should always be accessible to all; practice: he, the Vicar, had lost every key placed in his care since the age of seven. Since there was nothing much of value left in either church or vicarage the keys to both had become superfluous. Few members of the Parochial Church Council gave this argument much support, but the sentiment was heartily endorsed by every tramp in the district.

Since Trapp had been absent in what he called 'retreat' for the previous three weeks the locking of a gate that had never previously been locked did come as a matter of mild surprise. The appearance of a new lock on the same gate came as no surprise at all. People were always fixing new locks in his absence, and had been doing so ever since he could remember. They had also been presenting him with new keys. No doubt some optimist would shortly give him a key to this lock. Meantime eight feet of pitted stone wall represented a minor obstacle compared to some he had surmounted in time past – literally and metaphorically.

The gate was six feet high, and inset into a gap in the wall which topped it by two feet. Using gate and wall for hand and foot holds, with cassock hem tucked into belt, Timothy heaved himself over the obstacle, and dropped to the other side. The last part of this operation was less decorous than it might have been, and the incumbent of St John's, Mitchell Stoke, landed flat on his back, arms and legs flaying. 'Blast!' he exclaimed very loudly.

'Hoy, hoy! Hoy, hoy!' screamed untold numbers of
voices. There was a seeming thunder of many feet. Little
oriental figures, swarthy, half naked, threatening and
muscular, some holding picks, others brandishing shovels,
one, the obvious leader, waving a particularly lethal-looking
knife, raced down upon the Vicar and surrounded him as
he lay in a tangle on the ground. With a bound the leader
leaped upon his chest, pinning him to the ground. 'Who
are you?' demanded this most unexpected of assailants.

'I am the Vicar,' replied Timothy who, even in the
circumstances, had time to savour the incongruity of the
introduction. Then with a practised bodily contraction and
a well-timed heave, he sent his would-be captor flying over
his head and crashing into the wall.

CHAPTER II

'I'll not apologize again then,' said George Scarbuck with
an extra touch of a native Yorkshire accent intended to
emphasize sincerity. 'Lack of supervision, that's the crutch
of the matter,' he continued; the Vicar's eyebrows raised
a fraction. 'I reckon you gave better than you got. Those
little heathen have learned a lesson they'll not forget in a
hurry.'

This comment was hardly appropriate coming from the
confessed employer and assumed protector of those same
little heathen, but to Trapp it seemed exactly characteristic
of the speaker he had been assessing with increasing horror
for the half-hour or so that had elapsed since he had been set
upon by six apparently crazed Filipinos.

'It's unlikely they're actually heathen, you know, Scarbuck,' commented Major-General Sir Arthur Moonlight,
Bart, DSO. 'The Roman Catholic Church got at most of the
Filipinos years ago. Of course, your lot could be part of
the Islamic minority.' He implied from his tone that there
might in any case be little to choose between followers of

the Pope of Rome and those owing their allegiance to Mohammed. The Moonlights had long since found it politic to join the Established Church.

'Judging by the respect they show for the cloth I'd guess they're Mohammedans,' put in Trapp, looking ruefully at a long width of cassock hem that hung irregularly around his ankles. 'Catholic Filipinos might not have laid into a priest with quite so much enthusiasm.'

'They'll not lay into anyone, most of them, for a while,' said Scarbuck. 'I'll bet you've been an exhibitionist in your time, Vicar.' Trapp trusted he caught the speaker's meaning. 'The two you tackled might just be fit for work this afternoon. Let's hope so, anyway; I've got to pack the lot of them north tonight and home next Friday.'

The three men were seated in the study of the Dower House. The Vicar seemed wholly composed after his adventure which had culminated in the laying out of one further assailant and the retreat of four others, just as the curious figure of George Scarbuck had hurried on to the scene from the direction of Mitchell Hall. Scarbuck had introduced himself as the new owner of the Hall, a claim Trapp had found even more astonishing than the reception he had received after tumbling off the wall. The two had stood for a while to talk before walking across the garden front of the Hall to the Dower House – Trapp's original destination.

Scarbuck, a paunchy sixty, looked wholly unconvincing in the role of new lord and master of an Oxfordshire country estate (albeit a severely contracted one), and this in sharp contrast to the tall, text-book military appearance of the previous owner.

Sir Arthur Moonlight had succeeded to the title at the age of twenty-four. Already embarked on a successful career in the regular army, he had no taste for farming, and had found over the years that his progress as a military engineer was in no way complemented by the often necessarily remote control management of a fifteen-hundred-acre estate. He had in consequence sold all his farm land twenty years since to his not altogether grateful tenants who had found the price of fifty pounds an acre steep if not actually outrageous. Most of them had later discovered that milking the rich burghers of Reading and London was an infinitely more profitable pursuit than doing the same to Jersey cows, and had made impressive fortunes by dividing pasture land into large and desirable building plots. Indeed, the farmers having acquired a distinctly non-agrarian zeal for self if not local improvement, it was only the intervention of a prescient Government – and the predictable and outraged objections of the burghers by then *in situ* – that had prevented the later conversion of Mitchell Stoke into a minor metropolis. The farmers had subsequently returned to expensively equipped, mechanized husbandry, the burghers had arranged the construction of a golf-course, and Sir Arthur Moonlight had come to regret his initial benevolence.

Six years ago, Moonlight had retired from the army. A distinguished soldier, he was also a respected authority on the history of military architecture. The subject being one that had proved to be of less than consuming interest to contemporary historians, it could be said that Moonlight had cornered the market – such as it was – for commentaries on any aspect of his speciality that editors considered worthy of an airing. Even so, calls for enlightenment on the placement of Welsh castles or the distribution of Martello Towers were not matters of daily occurrence. Indeed, the General had seriously over-estimated the extra monies he had expected to enjoy in fees and royalties from his occasional lectures and writing. These proved to be hardly a significant supplement to the income from his capital and a service pension traditionally geared to the winter rates of south coast three-star hotels.

The ravages of inflation had so sadly decreased the value of his income from all sources that after three years Moonlight had decided to improve his lot by throwing open Mitchell Hall to what he had confidently assumed would be an eager public. This action proved as costly as it was disastrous.

After two seasons, Sir Arthur was obliged to cut the heavy losses in capital expenditure involved in completely redecorating and largely refurbishing the house. The seventy-eight persons who had up to that time seen fit to visit the premises at 50p a head had done little to compensate for the cost either of the interior improvements or the exterior additions. These had included an extensive car-park and other necessary amenities, although the Moonlights had stopped short of a fun-fair, a zoo, or any other kind of addition aimed at making a cultural expedition more digestible for common people. This was probably a mistake. In any event, Mitchell Hall had been put up for sale, and Arthur Moonlight and his wife Elizabeth had moved into the Dower House next door.

Sadly, the availability of one of Britain's least known country houses had not produced a charge of willing buyers. Twelve bedrooms and eight acres of Green Belt garden might have had their attractions in another age. But even the proximity of the M4 motorway and the existence of a spanking new, well-equipped ladies' and gentlemen's convenience behind the forecourt shrubbery had failed to enthuse either the property speculator or the rich industrialist searching for evidence of an impressive provenance.

The fact was that Mitchell Hall was too good to pull down, but not good enough to be worth maintaining. It was too large as a home, and too small for institutional use. And it had stuck.

In normal circumstances General Sir Arthur Moonlight would not have entertained the notion of suffering George Scarbuck as a neighbour, let alone as the purchaser of the ancestral home of the Moonlights. But circumstances were not normal. Mitchell Hall had been on the market for eighteen months without an offer from any source when Scarbuck appeared one morning in late March. After the most cursory tour of the premises, and without so much as a glance at the garden, he had offered Moonlight a cheque for £200,000 in return for immediate possession. Since this sum was £50,000 beyond Moonlight's wildest expectations he had accepted with alacrity, conscious that if he was obliged to repent at leisure, he could now afford to do so in some comfort.

The transaction had taken place only three weeks ago, but Scarbuck had clearly wasted no time in pursuing his intentions for Mitchell Hall.

'Anny and me are going to make this our real home,' he had explained to Timothy Trapp earlier, and immediately following the one-man rout of Scarbuck's private army. 'Anny's the wife; you'll meet her soon – not here yet though; place's not fit for a pig at the moment' – a comment presumably not intended to reflect adversely on Mrs Scarbuck, and one that in any case seemed curiously wide of the truth.

Trapp debated whether he could take all this as intimation that the new owner of Mitchell Hall intended to lop off the top floor or simply to convert the basement into a giant cocktail bar. His companion gave every appearance of being capable of either or worse excess. Scarbuck was draped in a red, white and blue blazer which erratically followed the design of the Union Jack. It had clearly taxed the ingenuity of some conscientious but singularly insensitive tailor to produce this outrageous article of clothing, which gave its wearer the appearance, in naval parlance, of being dressed over-all. In addition he wore a bow tie of similar design, and a cap of the type favoured by American golfers, also apparently fashioned from the National flag with the title FORWARD BRITAIN emblazoned in large gold letters above the peak.

'Mitchell Hall will soon become the centre for the Movement,' continued Scarbuck, and as though the meaning of this statement was self-evident went on, 'That's a dog and a half you've got there.'

A few minutes earlier Scarbuck had unlocked and opened the gate into the churchyard through which Bach had emerged in credible emulation of a racing greyhound in hot pursuit of a very fast-moving electric hare. He was now poised aggressively atop a massive mound of earth piled

just below the place where the orangery had stood, barking
fiercely at things in general because the scene offered too
much choice for him to single out anything in particular.
But if the sights and actions before him prompted loud
remark from the Vicar's dog, they were even more remarkable
to the Vicar himself.

The orangery had been replaced by a hole, the proportions
of which made Horace Worple's current excavation in the
graveyard look very small beer indeed. Forty feet long and
twenty feet wide – or so Trapp judged – the hole matched
the surface proportions of the eastern pavilion that occupied
the balancing site on the far side of the Hall from where he
and Scarbuck were standing. More Filipinos than had been
involved in the fracas were engaged in digging, shovelling
and transporting earth; some were fixing a lining of wooden
props around the inside of the deepening excavation, the
floor of which sloped downwards at the southern end. The
side nearest the churchyard wall was draped to its full
depth by a giant piece of tarpaulin.

Overseeing the whole antlike operation was a gaunt,
sallow-faced European dressed in blue overalls that would
have been several sizes too large for him had he not evidently
been wearing an overcoat as well as normal clothing underneath. As it was, the overalls produced a distinctly bell-
tentish effect around the man's upper thighs. He looked
unused to artisan's clothing, uncomfortable, and judging
from his expression, uneasy – all at the same time. He had
emerged from the Hall behind Scarbuck earlier, but had
not spoken to Trapp while supervising the removal of the
two dazed labourers and motioning the others back to work.
Now he was eyeing Bach from the north end of the hole with
undisguised distaste, as were all the diminutive labourers.
As the man turned to give an order in what appeared to
be sign language to one of the workers, Trapp noticed that
the words SCARBUCK CONSTRUCTION were stencilled
on the back of his overalls.

'Heel, Bach!' cried the Vicar, more in the hope than the
belief that the animal would pay the least attention. 'Biscuit!'

he added, this being the only summons guaranteed to produce
a response. The dog immediately abandoned an interest
which was in any case beginning to pall and bounded back to
his master. Timothy Trapp was often given to wishing that
the cry 'boiled beef and carrots' issued from the church
porch would bring parishioners to worship with equal
alacrity.

'It's a swimming pool,' volunteered Scarbuck, which
at least served to banish the thought from Trapp's mind that
open-cast mining had been started not ten yards from the
church's boundary. 'Ten feet at the deep end, ceramic
lining, it'll be a tidy job when it's done ... Anny likes a dip,
so do I, come to that. You get more buoyancy with depth.'

'The workers,' Trapp enquired, 'they're not – er – local?'

'No, they're not, they're Filipinos,' Scarbuck answered.
'I bring 'em over by charter plane, two hundred at a time on
a month's holiday as you might say.' This statement was
accompanied by a conspiratorial wink. 'Then off they go
home at the end of four weeks with fifty quid in their pockets;
fortune to them, that is. Grand little workers too; not skilled,
you understand, and don't speak a word of English, except
for the foreman that is, the one who jumped you, and he
only speaks "pidgin". These twelve are from a gang I've
got on a big site up north ... It's a fiddle really,' he ended,
in a tone that implied he thought it was nothing of the sort.

'You mean they're not supposed to work in this country.
The Government or somebody might object?'

'Well, that's it in theory,' replied Scarbuck, 'but who's
to know they're not tourists? Anyway, you can't get British
labourers for the mucky, low-paid jobs any more, and
"spades" take for ever.' He paused, then continued meaning-
fully, 'They'll stay here for ever too if we go on paying 'em
the earth.'

It took a moment for Trapp to work out from these last
remarks that Scarbuck considered coloured immigrants were
slow workers, and in his opinion undesirable residents. The
nature of the FORWARD BRITAIN movement began to take
shape in the mind of the honorary chaplain to the Oxford-

shire branch of the Race Relations Committee.

'Careful little chaps too,' continued Scarbuck, unaware of the seeds of hostility he was sowing in the mind of his clerical companion. 'On a job like this you may need delicate handling now and again. Valuable bits and pieces come out of historical 'oles; it's not work for bull-dozers. We've got nowt of value here so far but you never can tell. That's why I've got Eustace Dankton on the job.' He nodded towards the sorrowful figure in overalls. 'Doesn't know a pick from a shovel, that one,' Scarbuck continued, 'but he's the right man to have around this site. Very distinguished antiquararian and bible-ographer.' Scarbuck had brought off a double. 'Ever heard of him?'

Trapp shook his head.

'No, well, perhaps he's not as famous as he makes out. The fuss he kicks up having to stand about while this is going on, you'd think he was Sir Mortimer Whatsit. He just came in to complain before you landed off the wall. Anyroad, he'll have to stay there the rest of the morning while Johnnie – he's the foreman – gets over that tumble you gave him.'

'I'm sorry about that, but . . .' Trapp began.

'It's not for you to be sorry, Vicar. In fact I take it very kindly you're not prosecuting for assault with a deadly weapon.' Scarbuck paused. 'You're not, are you?'

'Of course not,' replied the Vicar, who had returned the night before from three weeks field training with a unit of Royal Marine Commandos – an uncommon form of 'retreat' for a country parson, and one that in this case fortunately revived skills not normally required for safe progress on the broadwalks of English country houses.

'Good,' said Scarbuck, evidently much relieved. 'Fact is, there are a lot of queer customers about this village at the moment and Johnnie's been told to warn off strangers – not with a knife, you understand. He exceeded orders there; wouldn't have happened if Dankton had been at his post. Silly sod. Oh, sorry, Vicar,' he added hurriedly, glaring with deepened disapproval at his cultural adviser, who Trapp imagined must be drawing very handsome compensation indeed for the insults as well as the inconvenience he appeared to be suffering.

'By the way, that's the reason I've had a new lock put on that gate – the trespassers, I mean,' continued Scarbuck. Trapp waited for the promise he knew must follow. 'I'll let you have a key,' said Scarbuck and then, unexpectedly, 'in a day or two.' So sentence was delayed.

'Please don't trouble,' pleaded the Vicar with more sincerity than Scarbuck was likely to credit. 'It's really just as easy for me to get to the Dower House by the road.'

This statement had been patently untrue. The church, Mitchell Hall, and the Dower House lay in a straight line running east, in that order, set back from the main street of the village. The church occupied a corner site. Below it the road turned left to run parallel with the river, though some two hundred yards from its bank. The vicarage lay next to the church around the bend in the road. In calling on the Moonlights the Vicar had invariably used a roughly diagonal route through the churchyard. With the Hall unoccupied, the walk from his garden, through the church-yard, and across the garden front of the Hall had been as agreeable as it had been convenient. As he continued this way with the embarrassingly conspicuous Scarbuck at his side, he resolved to go by the road in future.

As they had entered the Dower House, Trapp had been curious to observe what kind of reception Moonlight would offer the new owner of Mitchell Hall. It proved to be warmer than he expected, though Moonlight who was usually relaxed and self-possessed showed a mild apprehension in his manner. Trapp had thought this probably a normal enough reaction in persons confronted by the curiously adorned Scarbuck. Even so, it appeared that Scarbuck had been expected, though he had not mentioned the fact on the way. Thus it was that Trapp felt he might be intruding. Bach showed no misgivings about the extent of the welcome due to him. After a short re-familiarization tour of the study, he settled at Moonlight's feet – a considered act of flattery which he invariably employed in houses where the floor coverings were softer than those at the Vicarage.

Following the exchange on the subject of Trapp's earlier adventure with the Filipinos, neither Moonlight nor Scarbuck made reference to the reason for their meeting. Trapp was thus prompted to get his own small business over and to depart. 'The funeral service for Maggie Edwards will be at two-thirty,' he said, addressing Moonlight. 'I wondered whether you might like . . .'

'Of course we'll be there, Timothy,' put in Moonlight. 'Most unfortunate. I suppose she'll be sadly missed in the village. Heart attack. Very sudden.' He looked down at the pipe he was grooving.

'Yes,' said Trapp carefully. 'I suppose that's what it was – brought on by over-exertion. She was tidying up the grass around the Acropolis; probably overdid it for a woman of her age, collapsed and died. But I was forgetting, it was Lady Elizabeth who found her, wasn't it? – or so Mrs Banquet told me.'

The lady last named was invariably the principal and first messenger of gloomy tidings in the life of Timothy Trapp. Mrs Banquet was his non-resident housekeeper who arrived at the vicarage each day shortly after breakfast for three hours, returning for a shorter session after lunch. This was a mutually convenient arrangement. Mr Banquet, a man of few words – most of them unprintable – was gardener at several houses in the vicinity. His loquacious wife had been delighted to 'oblige the Vicar, poor soul', as she put it, since with two sons grown up and departed the family home, she had time on her hands. From experience in two former parishes, Trapp preferred not to have a housekeeper live in, and since engaging Mrs Banquet his resolve in this connection had strengthened.

On his return from Exeter the previous evening, Mrs Banquet had related the tale of Maggie Edwards's demise in such detail one might have assumed she had been present during the whole unhappy event which, it appeared, had been witnessed by no one. In a spirit of Christian helpfulness, Maggie had been for many years self-appointed, unpaid keeper of the churchyard pathways. This involved no more than clipping the grass edges but it was a task she carried on regularly from spring to autumn – a valuable supplement to the twice-yearly scything of the churchyard grass which Horace Worple undertook on a strictly stipendiary basis.

The Acropolis referred to by Trapp was the title commonly given by local people to the monument to the first baronet: it was a miniature reproduction of a Roman temple-tomb. Erected by the second baronet in 1630, some years before the building of Mitchell Hall, it stood as better testimony to his genuine regard for classical architecture than did the house itself. Situated mid-way between the largely Gothic church and the mannerist Hall, the monument was as pleasing as it was unexpected. Maggie Edwards had taken a special delight in keeping its surrounds free of weeds and grass, but at the last her enthusiasm appeared to have been her undoing. At some time on the previous Tuesday afternoon she had collapsed and died beside the Acropolis. Her body had not been discovered until some hours later when Lady Moonlight had been returning through the churchyard from a walk by the river.

'There had to be a post mortem, of course,' said Moonlight. 'Cardiac arrest, I think they said. Nasty experience for Elizabeth.'

Trapp nodded. 'According to the imaginative Mrs Banquet,' he observed, 'Maggie died of shock.'

Neither of the other two men spoke.

CHAPTER III

Mark Treasure slowed the Rolls-Royce to seventy miles an hour. The feeling of virtue that this induced was without justification since the car had been doing ninety for all of twenty miles. Exit 12 of the Motorway was less than half a mile ahead, which put Mitchell Stoke only twenty minutes away.

It was ten-thirty on a sunny Saturday morning in April, and the Vice-Chairman of Grenwood, Phipps & Co., respected merchant bankers, reverted to savouring the pleasure of the day and the contentments in store – a train of thought that had been earlier interrupted by the need to concentrate on the sighting of police cars.

Meetings that Treasure had been committed to begin that day in Kuwait had been cancelled at short notice. Thus, late on the previous afternoon he had enjoyed the luxury of debating ways in which he might employ the unexpectedly free days ahead. Because he was naturally industrious – and temporarily wifeless – it was to his credit that most of his plans had involved work as well as pleasure. This definition might even have been extended (without the credit) to include a momentary fantasy – swiftly dismissed – involving a singularly attractive female graduate from the Research Department. On coming to retrieve an unrequired report on the Middle East the girl had proffered a remark about his now being free to enjoy a proper weekend in England. An instinctive conclusion – in fact correct – that this might constitute an invitation to enjoy it improperly in South Kensington had been an agreeable boost to Treasure's ego. The prudent decision not to test the speculation had nearly been rationalized into an iron conviction that he had no wish to try when the telephone had rung. It was Arthur Moonlight.

'Come for the weekend, or longer if you can manage it. You can get in some golf, give me some advice, and cheer up Elizabeth,' Moonlight had said. And so the matter had been resolved.

Treasure and Elizabeth Moonlight were second cousins, and more or less of an age – both a good deal younger than Moonlight himself, who had not married until his mid-thirties. Treasure valued his friendship with the couple and seldom refused an opportunity to be in their company.

Tall, good-looking, amusing and first-rate at his work, Treasure combined the attributes of the traditional, inspired amateur in merchant banking with latter-day tutored professionalism. He owed this to necessity since he had not been born into banking. It was said that he had talked his way into Grenwood, Phipps helped by a good degree and a Half-blue for golf. It had taken him a good deal less than the twenty years he had been with the company to prove that he relied on more than light-hearted verbosity to produce the right results. Now at the wheel of the expensive car that he owned but too seldom drove himself, he might have been mistaken for a maturing but successful actor. This was why the short, jolly-looking young woman begging a lift on the A340 road hardly expected him to stop; but he did.

'I say, awfully good of you,' she cried heartily through the near-side window which Treasure was lowering by remote control. Slightly confused by her unexpected good fortune and a trifle breathless from her short run after the Rolls, she detached herself from the over-sized knapsack on her back. 'Might I chuck the papoose in the back d'you think?' Treasure smiled and nodded, unlocking the rear door with the master switch at his right hand. 'I say, what an absolutely super car,' said his new companion settling herself into the front seat beside him. 'Do the seats eject as well?' She gave a short, nervous laugh.

'Only after take-off,' said Treasure gravely. 'Meantime you can adjust yours in most directions electrically with that little knob.'

'No, honestly?' said the girl in evident awe, but she made no move to operate the gadgetry despite the fact that due to her height, and the set of the seat, half her view from the car was obstructed by the dashboard. Instead she gave Treasure what he took to be a look of frank appraisal.

'Goodbody,' she said.

Treasure was used to compliments but not to gratuitous carnal assessments from strange young women. 'Thelma Goodbody,' she continued, thrusting out a chubby hand evidently for shaking.

Treasure felt relieved, if a shade disappointed. 'How d'you do,' he said. 'My name's Mark Treasure and I'm head-

ing for Mitchell Stoke. Is that on your route?' He set the
car moving.

'What a bit of luck,' exclaimed Miss Goodbody. 'That's
exactly where I'm going . . . well, almost. I'm making for
The Jolly Boatman at Binford, that's straight across the
river from Mitchell Stoke, and I can go over on the chain
ferry.'

'Yes, I've known that ferry since before you were born,'
said Treasure who figured Miss Goodbody was in her early
twenties. 'So it's still working?'

'Well, it was the day before yesterday,' she replied with a
smile. 'I'm using it a lot. You see, I'm doing some research
work at Mitchell Stoke – on the church and the Hall.
Really I should be staying in the village but the pub there's
a bit pricey, and I gather the food's not startling either.'

Treasure agreed with this assessment of The Bell at
Mitchell Stoke, a very over-rated riverside hotel which had
become undeservedly popular after tasteless 'modernization'
in the 'fifties. 'What sort of research are you doing?' he
asked.

'Oh, literary,' replied Miss Goodbody. 'I was jolly lucky
to get a postgraduate grant last year to work for a doctorate.'
She swayed forward in a contorted gesture of embarrassment
involving contraction of neck, arms and legs. This so reduced
her physical contact with the seat that Treasure feared she
might roll off. 'I'm not good enough really, but I'm having
a go. My subject's Shakespeare. He's awfully overdone, of
course.'

'So which bit of him are you doing again?' asked Treasure.

'Well, I'm writing a paper on first nights, trial performances, that sort of thing. The plays were altered a lot, you
know, by Shakespeare himself and the actors – sort of as
they went along. And they had a kind of provincial circuit,
mostly country houses, for repertory *and* new pieces. Of
course the evidence is terribly slim,' she ended apologetically.

'But you're fattening it up,' said Treasure encouragingly.

'Yes,' she replied with great enthusiasm. 'I've been all
over the place – travelling mostly by bus; bit different from

your car.' Miss Goodbody was contracting again.

Treasure put in quickly, 'And where does Mitchell Stoke come in?'

'Oh, *As You Like It* was probably done there – at least I think so. It was certainly done at Wilton, possibly before London. Nobody knows the dates. There was no quarto printed, and the play wasn't properly registered at Stationer's Hall. That's where I was yesterday.' And, as if evidence of industry were required: 'As well as the British Museum.' Miss Goodbody was getting into her stride. 'They *think* Shakespeare wrote it in 1599. Of course, it's a terribly open-air sort of play; orchards and forests – that sort of thing – so he could have written it specially for performing outdoors in people's gardens – don't you think?' she added uncertainly.

Treasure hoped that the basis of Miss Goodbody's research was bedded in something stronger than the opinions of chance acquaintances like himself. His knowledge of Shakespeare was limited. True, some years before, his wife had done a season with the Royal Shakespeare and he had loyally attended three times to watch what the critics had described as her definitive characterization of Portia in *The Merchant*. He recalled, too, having seen *As You Like It* performed in a college garden when he was an undergraduate.

'I should think that's a quite tenable theory,' he replied, but with a degree of guardedness his City acquaintances would have considered labelled the proposition as most probably spurious. Miss Goodbody was an unsuspecting innocent in this context. 'But what makes the garden of Mitchell Hall a front runner?'

'Well,' said Miss Goodbody in a conspiratorial tone, 'two reasons – and one was just jolly good luck. Have you heard of Eustace Dankton?'

'No,' Treasure replied, thereby and inadvertently being the second agent in one morning to question that person's entitlement to the fame that some ascribed to him. 'Should I have?'

'I suppose not,' said Miss Goodbody, 'but he's quite well known in his own field. He's what I'd like to be – a sort of rummager round of old houses looking for ancient documents. He's made several quite important "finds" in the libraries of stately homes. Just recently he found something actually in the wall of a house that was being knocked down near Northampton. It's terribly exciting work really. Gosh, that was good driving.'

Treasure credited the last remark to cool nerves. He had just overtaken a lorry they had been trailing for several miles on a tight stretch of road, in the process narrowly missing a collision with a small yellow car coming from the opposite direction, and at a speed that he considered illegal for all drivers save himself and the very few others who would employ it with discretion. He also determined to continue the journey at a more decorous pace; if necessary, behind slow-moving lorries. The consequences of getting killed with Miss Goodbody would be embarrassing as well as inconvenient. He glanced at his passenger; though distinctly plump, she was comely, and attractive enough to be potentially compromising. 'Banker and girl die in Rolls' – he could think of at least one business partner whose sorrow would be tinged with uncharitable doubt. Miss Goodbody smiled back at him, unconscious of his morbid train of thought and the relative compliment it suggested.

'Anyway,' she continued enthusiastically, 'Mr Dankton did a paper on this Northampton discovery about three months ago. He found a diary, or part of a diary, kept during the Civil War by the father of Sarah Moonlight – she was married to the second baronet Moonlight of Mitchell Stoke. The Moonlights have been lords of the manor there for centuries . . .'

'I'm on my way to stay with them now,' Treasure interrupted.

'Gosh,' said Miss Goodbody, obviously impressed, 'they're absolutely super people, and terribly helpful. I cornered Sir Arthur after a lecture he gave to the History Society in Oxford last term – bit of a cheek really, but he was sweet; said I could go over the Moonlight library any time. Only trouble is, there's not much of it left. Sir Arthur and his wife moved out of the Hall some time ago – but you probably know all about that?'

'Yes,' replied Treasure, 'and they had more furniture and books and things than they knew what to do with – the Dower House is quite large but they still had to let go lots of their things. A good many of the books went to university libraries. But you still haven't told me what was in this diary.'

'Well, it's all jolly sad really,' continued Miss Goodbody. 'Poor Sarah sort of took refuge with her parents when the war was at its height. Her father writes about her grief at leaving her gorgeous new home and her loving husband, in that order by the way. She was even more cut up at having to drop the plans she had for widening the artistic life they were leading. And that's the bit that Mr Dankton finds significant. There's evidence in other parts of the diary that Sarah, even more than her husband, had ambitions about being a noted patron of the arts, and that very much included the theatre – carrying on the tradition started by the first baronet. Well, you couldn't talk about starting a tradition for theatrical patronage at the beginning of the seventeenth century without having *something* to do with Shakespeare, and the Moonlights *were* friends of the Pembrokes at Wilton. And that was my first clue.' Miss Goodbody treated herself to a modest smile of satisfaction. 'Then I got a stroke of the sheerest good luck when Timothy Trapp was made Vicar of Mitchell Stoke; bit of luck for him too, as a matter of fact.'

'I knew about the appointment,' said Treasure, slowing down the car at a junction in the middle of Pangbourne. 'So you know the new incumbent? I haven't met him yet.'

'But Timothy's famous,' said Miss Goodbody, as if to suggest that it was only a matter of time before the worthy Trapp was translated to Canterbury, 'though I suppose some people would say infamous' – which detracted something from the firmness of the first remark. 'You see, he's a dedicated Christian.'

Treasure was sufficiently acquainted with the inner workings of the Church of England to appreciate that the

overt practice of Christian principles on the part of one of
its clergy could, in certain circumstances, lead to embarrassment, but he found the charge of infamy a likely over-
statement levelled at the incumbent of a living in the sole
gift of Arthur Moonlight. 'Mr Trapp is a friend of yours?'
he enquired.

'Well, he was my brother's friend first,' replied Miss
Goodbody. 'They were at the same college, and Timothy
used to stay with us in the vacations. After university he
joined the Royal Marine Commandos, terribly dashing and
exciting. Then he suddenly chucked it, and went into a
theological college.'

'You mean he found a latish vocation to be a priest,'
said Treasure.

'Something like that,' the girl replied, 'but they got more
than they bargained for when they got Timothy. You see,
he really lives the life – and it gets him into terrible trouble
one way and another.'

'You mean he's excessively holy?' Treasure was not yet
certain he was going to enjoy making the acquaintance of
Timothy Trapp.

'Oh, not in a "pi" sense,' Miss Goodbody protested.
'He's just . . . well, a priest who practises what he preaches
in an everyday sort of way. In his last living, it was in a
run-down part of Bristol, he sold all the church plate – it
was terribly valuable – to build a home for unmarried
mothers. There was an awful row when the authorities found
out, and the Church Commissioners had to buy back the
plate to save everybody's face. But by that time the building
was finished.'

'But surely the plate was missed,' commented Treasure,
'and in any case church treasures are left in trust to successive
generations, not, as it were, at the disposal of passing
clergymen.' His sense of moral values made him quite
certain of the validity of this statement, even if it did sound
pompous.

'It wasn't missed because nobody ever saw it,' replied
Miss Goodbody. 'It was in a bank vault, and had been for

years. Most of it had been presented to the church by rich
merchant adventurers in the eighteenth and nineteenth
centuries. Timothy argued they'd probably made their
money out of slave trading anyway, so the Church shouldn't
have accepted their gifts in the first place.'

Treasure wondered how many of the Church's riches
stored up in England would stand justification against this
kind of criterion. 'Your Mr Trapp sounds as if he's set to
take on the whole Establishment with ideas like that,' he
observed.

'*Father* Trapp, actually,' replied Miss Goodbody. 'He's
terribly High Church. But the Establishment's winning. He's
been sort of "moved on" from two livings already as well as
from his first curacy. *They* didn't go for him because he
refused to read prayers about stopping the war in Vietnam.'

'You mean he approved of the war in Vietnam?' Treasure
found this proposition hard to credit.

'Oh no,' said Father Trapp's champion. 'He felt that asking
God to stop a war suggested to people that God started it
in the first place, and that both suggestions were wrong and
irreligious. I think he's right too.'

Treasure began to wonder how long the worthy Trapp
was likely to survive in Holy Orders. 'Doesn't Father Trapp
have a little difficulty in finding employment?' he asked.

'More than a little,' Miss Goodbody agreed, 'but the
Bishop of Oxford has known him since he was an ordinand
and he's rescued Timothy a couple of times already. After
Bristol he made Timothy promise to spend a few years
thinking, not doing – you know, kind of sorting out his
philosophy. If Timothy co-operated then the Bishop said
he would help find him a country parish where he could sort
of contemplate for a bit – and that's where Sir Arthur Moonlight came in. The Mitchell Stoke living is in his gift, you
know – ' Treasure did know – 'and Sir Arthur was willing
to take on Timothy because the Bishop thinks priests like
him should be kept in the Church, not chucked out because
they have original ideas,' she ended almost defiantly.

Treasure made a mental note to enquire the whereabouts

of any valuables belonging to St John's, Mitchell Stoke, though he assumed – correctly – that Moonlight, being forewarned, would also have been forearmed against the eccentricities of his ecclesiastical protégé.

'And in the process of "sorting out his philosophy", your Timothy has also found out something about Shakespeare?' he enquired.

'I wish he was my Timothy.' Miss Goodbody blushed to the roots of her mousey hair, and Treasure was prompted to wonder whether academic research was the sole reason for her interest in Mitchell Stoke. 'But yes, he did hit on something marvellous and wrote to me about it. In the May of 1599 the local carpenter had triplets – or rather his wife did – all boys, and they were christened Oliver, Jaques and Orlando. What d'you think of that?' Miss Goodbody beamed at Treasure with the air of a conjuror who had just completed a particularly difficult hat trick.

'Fancy,' said Treasure, conscious only that the names had a Shakespearean ring about them.

Aware that the staggering information she had just imparted had been received with something less than astonishment, Miss Goodbody continued: 'Those were the names given to the three sons of Sir Rowland de Boys in *As You Like It*. Don't you see, the coincidence is too clear really to be a coincidence. The names are not even common English ones. They must have been taken from the play, but so far as anyone knows the play hadn't been performed anywhere before the late summer of 1599.'

Treasure began to understand the drift of Miss Goodbody's argument, and the reason for her obvious excitement. 'You mean you believe the village carpenter at Mitchell Stoke had seen the play before his wife presented him with triplets, and that it's not very likely he was a regular attendant at the Globe Theatre in London?' He felt this minimum deductive offering on his part at least established him as something better than an academic moron in the face of such inventive scholarship.

'Exactly,' replied Miss Goodbody triumphantly, 'or

almost exactly anyway,' she continued, implying that either Treasure was jumping to his conclusions, or else that she exercised a more disciplined approach to hers. 'What we know for a fact,' she continued, 'is that the triplets were baptized on 6 May 1599 – that's what Timothy unearthed in the Parish Register. What it's reasonable to suppose is that if a band of travelling players visited Mitchell Stoke in that year the local craftsman most likely to have been involved with them was the carpenter . . .'

'Even though the play was performed in the open air,' Treasure put in, not wishing to be outdone if exactitude was to be questioned.

'True,' Miss Goodbody nodded, 'because even an open-air performance requires something in the way of rudimentary sets – things like screens, benches, and so on. Just imagine, one of Shakespeare's plays may have been staged for the very first time in this village.' They had just entered Mitchell Stoke. 'Golly, if only I can prove it.'

CHAPTER IV

'I can't imagine anything truly alarming happening in our churchyard at three o'clock in the afternoon,' Trapp volunteered. He sensed, but could not understand, the tenseness his earlier remark had caused. 'Apparently Maggie did have a very weak heart,' he added rather lamely.

'P'raps a mouse ran up her leg,' offered Scarbuck in a tone of forced bonhomie. 'There must be plenty of those in country churchyards.'

The only audible response to this unlikely conjecture was the sound of Moonlight blowing through the pipe he had been cleaning. 'Where are you putting Maggie?' he enquired in a quiet voice.

'She'll be breaking old ground this side of the church,' said Trapp. 'It's a part of the churchyard that hasn't been used for burials for something like two centuries, judging by the few gravestones that survive there. The churchwardens have come to the conclusion that that's a decent enough interval. Fact is there's no room left anywhere else.'

'You mean the patch between the Hall gate and the Acropolis,' Moonlight observed. Scarbuck stood up with such alacrity as to suggest he had been propelled by a powerful force outside his own control.

Trapp resisted an involuntary reflex to salute the flag. 'That's it,' he replied. 'Worple was hard at it when I came over – and hard's the word. He claimed he'd hit rock.'

'Not rock; stone more likely,' said Moonlight. 'The same stone the wall is made from. He's hit on a bit of the old Hall I should think. Solid stuff too. Eleventh-century monasteries were built to last – not many of them have, of course, except for what's underground.'

Scarbuck was doing his best to disguise a nevertheless evident state of agitation. He glanced at his watch for the second time in ten seconds, during which period he had been moving backwards towards the door of the study. 'You must forgive me, both of you,' he said. 'I've a date on site at eleven and it's gone that now. Nice to have met you, Vicar. Have a good . . . er . . . I hope the funeral goes all right.' And with that he hurried through the door and was gone.

'What an extraordinary man,' observed Trapp as soon as the door was safely closed.

'Repulsive little squirt would be more apposite,' said Moonlight, 'but then you're a charitable chap, Timothy.'

'Yes, but as a matter of fact, some of the things he said to me before we joined you were a bit of a strain. Does he wear those clothes all the time?'

'I should think it extremely likely he has a dressing-gown and pyjamas to match – or perhaps a nightshirt; the effect must be dazzling,' Moonlight replied. 'To be accurate, I think we got the total ensemble this morning because he's got a bus load of his followers arriving after lunch.'

'What, all dressed like that?'

'I've really no idea,' said Moonlight, 'but we shall no doubt find out later. Perhaps they'll all do a war dance around the swimming pool. Hope they fall in.'

'Exactly what is the Forward Britain Movement?' asked
Trapp. 'To be honest, I've never heard of it.'

'Then your ignorance does you credit, my boy. They're
somewhere to the right of Genghis Khan – anti-black,
anti-semitic, anti-Common Market, the lot. Little Englanders
with the accent on the little. Thank God they don't own a
gun-boat. Incidentally, how was your rest cure with the
gallant Commandos?'

'Invigorating, but I think it's time I gave it up. I'm
getting too old for scaling cliffs. Still, brushing up unarmed
combat was a useful exercise – I just wish the average Royal
Marine was as pint-sized as those little chaps who weighed
into me this morning. Well, I must be going.' Trapp made to
rise from his chair when the door opened and a smiling
Elizabeth Moonlight came into the room.

'Darling Timothy,' she exclaimed, 'how very good to have
you back, and here's another gorgeous man come to see
us.' Mark Treasure appeared in the doorway behind her.

Elizabeth Moonlight had lost little of the radiance, and
indeed natural beauty, that had made Arthur Moonlight
the envy of all his contemporaries when he had married her
twenty-odd years before. Simply, she had mellowed hand-
somely, kept her figure, her tiptilted nose, and her ability
to be totally engaging to men she considered worthy of
engaging. She was petite, very English, unmistakably
upper-crust, and not in the least ashamed of it. Timothy
Trapp adored her, but no more than did Mark Treasure.
Nor was there any circumstance that suited Elizabeth better
than to be in the company of three men who in their own
ways each made her feel younger and more attractive than
she really was.

When introductions had been completed, Elizabeth
poured coffee for the whole party from the trolley which
Treasure had been detailed to tow in behind him when he
first appeared. 'Timothy,' she said, 'have they told you
about my ghastly experience in the churchyard?' and without
waiting for a reply, 'Mark, there I was gliding between the

graves, a vision in last year's sheepskin, and, my dear, I
practically fall over a dead body. My poor Miss Edwards
had dropped dead right there on the path.'

Use of the possessive pronoun applied to the people she
liked was characteristic of Elizabeth Moonlight. Few if any
of those that she thus appropriated felt anything but flattery
at being alluded to in this way. Maggie Edwards would
have been no exception, and with good reason. Even though
the Moonlights had been obliged to divest themselves of
more and more of their worldly possessions, they had never
considered abandoning what both regarded as the obligations
of rank. They were much involved in the well-being of the
inhabitants of what they termed the 'old village'. The spirit
of *noblesse oblige* was still very much alive in the Moonlights.

'And what I shall never forget was the look on her face,'
Elizabeth continued. 'She was petrified – well, perhaps that's
the wrong word, more . . . er . . . horrified. Yes, that's it; as
though she'd been frightened to death.'

'A heart attack can be very frightening, my dear,' said
Moonlight firmly.

'Yes, but somehow one doesn't expect people to look
anything but reposed in death,' Elizabeth replied. 'Not that
I've seen many dead people. Aunt Mildred I remember
looked rather smug, as if she'd just had the last laugh – she
had too, leaving all her money to the RSPCA. We'll come
to the funeral of course, Timothy – two-thirty, isn't it?'

'I'm sure that will be appreciated by the relatives,' Trapp
replied. 'I gather there are some, coming from London.
Sorry to deprive you of your hosts, Mr Treasure, but the
service will barely last half an hour.'

'I shan't mind in the very least,' said Treasure. 'And
please call me Mark. As a matter of fact I have a date at
two-thirty with your ardent admirer Miss Goodbody.' He
then related the story of his morning encounter, and how he
had engaged to accompany Miss Goodbody on a hopeful
journey of detection later in the day. 'Mark you, Timothy,'
he ended, adopting the familiar address that seemed appropriate, 'I'm sure she'd rather have you for company.'

Trapp smirked self-consciously. 'I did offer to put her up at the vicarage,' he said, 'but she insisted it would compromise me. Thelma observes all the old-fashioned niceties.' Treasure considered that Timothy Trapp perhaps underestimated Miss Goodbody's particular regard for his reputation.

'D'you really believe this Shakespeare business, Mark?' Elizabeth enquired. 'Timothy's been on about it ever since he unearthed those parish registers, but Arthur is distinctly sceptical.'

'Not sceptical, just realistic,' put in Moonlight. 'The evidence so far is slim, and I see no possibility of anyone finding any more.'

'But the concept is exciting,' said Treasure. 'Just imagine Mitchell Stoke becoming a minor Stratford-on-Avon. You'd be on the American travel agents' itineraries in no time.'

'A bit late for that,' said Moonlight ruminatively.

'Yes,' Elizabeth broke in, 'and we could have Molly here doing a summer season on the lawn. Mark, how is Molly, you haven't told us? Is the American play a success?'

'A wild one, I gather.' Treasure wished it were not so, since his wife had already been in New York for three months. 'The thing should run for six months at least, and it's really only the most trifling domestic comedy. A season here in Shakespeare would probably be very good for her art.'

'Well, we could hardly recreate the original setting,' Moonlight observed. 'The old Hall has gone, and whatever they had for a garden with it.'

'Of course, the old Hall – the monastery building – was in quite a different position from the present Hall,' said Trapp.

'Yes,' Moonlight said, 'it was much closer to the church, on the patch of rising ground that leads up to the wall. It became part of the graveyard when the new building was finished on the high ground to the east.' He paused. 'The monastery was stone built, not brick like the Hall. There are several cottages in the village made up from the old materials – you must have noticed them. The wall itself, of course, was salvaged stone. I always thought they must have dumped the subsoil from the foundations of the new Hall on the site of the old one because the ground rises quite steeply from the Acropolis eastwards. There's no trace of the old Hall left, though Timothy was saying earlier that our gravedigger appears to have unearthed a bit this morning.' He glanced at Trapp. 'D'you know how deep he was, Timothy?'

'Seven foot six,' replied the Vicar with a firmness and accuracy that surprised his hearers. He smiled. 'Worple told me so.'

'Isn't that deep for a grave?' asked Treasure.

'Ah, our Mr Worple likes to give value,' said Elizabeth, 'but have you seen how deep those jolly little Filipinos are going with Mr Scarbuck's swimming pool?' Moonlight and Trapp exchanged glances.

'Jolly is hardly the word after Timothy's experience this morning,' Moonlight told his wife. He followed with the story of Trapp's adventure.

'But how utterly preposterous,' Elizabeth protested. 'That dreadful little man should be reported to the police or the immigration authorities – or both.'

'So it's *that* Scarbuck who's bought the Hall,' Treasure put in.

'Why, d'you know him?' Moonlight asked quickly.

'Know of him,' his friend replied, 'and that frankly is as close as I'd care to get. But whatever possessed you . . .' He paused, obviously embarrassed. 'That wasn't Scarbuck who was leaving the house as I arrived – small, fat chap wrapped up in a Union Jack? I thought he must be out of a circus.'

'That was Scarbuck,' said Moonlight, 'and as for what possessed me to sell him the Hall, Elizabeth knows already, and Timothy must have guessed: we needed the money.'

There was a momentary silence, broken by Trapp who said, 'Now I really must go or I shall be keeping the Bishop

waiting. He's coming round to the vicarage at twelve to
give me what he calls an account of his stewardship. He's
got three weeks' collections banked but I don't suppose they'll
put the Church of England on a new financial footing.'
Bishop Clarence Wringle lived in retirement with his wife
Clara in a cottage close to the village. A self-styled 'ecclesiastical spare part', he acted as unpaid curate at St John's and
during Trapp's recent absence as stand-in Vicar.

Trapp heaved himself out of his chair, an action Bach
pretended to ignore.

'So you'll come for dinner tonight, Timothy,' said
Elizabeth firmly. 'Seven o'clock. And bring that cassock
with you, or else drop it in this afternoon and I'll mend it.
Scalloped hems are definitely out this year. The Wringles
are coming too, and I'm just going to ring Thelma Goodbody
at The Boatman to see if she's free – nice girl, if a trifle
hearty. Anyway, she's stimulating in a wholesome way.'
She gave all three men a satisfied glance as if to suggest that
other sorts of female stimulation might be bad for them.
'Come on then, Timothy, there's a bone in the kitchen
that Bach can take home.'

This last remark she had addressed in the direction of
the recumbent retriever, whose ability to sort out the words
that mattered from a general conversation brought him
promptly to Elizabeth's side as she and Trapp left the study.

The two men were left standing, facing each other.
Moonlight let out a deep sigh. 'Mark, I've made the most
ghastly error. The Hall. I've got to buy it back from that
evil man.'

'Oh come, he's not as bad as all that surely?' replied
Treasure. 'I wouldn't fancy him for a neighbour myself,
but the deed's done. Why not just plant a cupressus hedge
between here and the Hall? Then in a year or two you can
forget he's there. Out of sight out of mind.'

'The deed isn't done – well, not completely. I've taken
the fellow's money – come to that, I've spent some of it –
but the conveyancing business isn't complete. I'd hoped you
could advise me about putting the thing in reverse.'

'Well, I'm a banker not an estate agent,' said Treasure half jokingly. 'Still, if you're really serious . . . but if ownership hasn't been conveyed, does Scarbuck have the right to be doing all this digging you were talking about?'

'I've signed a preliminary deed of sale that gives him ownership of the Hall and everything in it. The thing is subject to proof of title before completion.'

'Then I imagine you have no right to withdraw at this stage, Arthur. I suppose you could make him an offer above what he's paid you. D'you want to tell me how much that was?'

'Two hundred thousand. Half of it was wiped out the day I got it – money I owed the bank for doing up the Hall and later this place and . . . er . . . other things. Financially I've been in a muddle for years. Selling the Hall was manna from heaven.'

'And now you want it back. But what are you going to do with it if you get it? And in any case, from what you say it doesn't sound as if you can afford it. Forgive me, Arthur, but you must be mad.'

Moonlight had walked to a window that looked out on to the Hall in the middle distance. He turned to face Treasure once again. 'I tell you, Mark, I'll go mad if I don't get the place back from that devil.' He paused. 'I've worked it out: if I realize all my assets, sell everything of value here including the house, I could probably scrape together a quarter of a million. I'll need a bit of bridging . . .'

'Which of course I could arrange. But what are you and Elizabeth going to live on afterwards, for heaven's sake? Be reasonable, Arthur: the Hall can't mean that much to you or you wouldn't have put it up for sale in the first place.'

'Mark, I want it back. I had the chap here this morning to make him an offer but he left before I had the chance. Will you do it for me? Will you get hold of him and make him sell?' Moonlight looked suddenly older and dejected. 'Normally I wouldn't ask such a thing, even from an old friend, but, Mark, something's happened and I'm desperate.

For God's sake help me get rid of that little swine.'

Timothy Trapp knelt piously in the vicarage cellar. This
was not a part of the house he reserved for his devotions,
and since he was humming 'Colonel Bogey' it would have
been evident even to the least informed observer that he
was not engaged in prayer. Here, though, he was safe from
Mrs Banquet, who regarded subterranean regions as below
the cleaning line. The cellar's contents if not its location
went some way to support this attitude. Successive incum-
bents had clearly used it as a depository for unwanted or
outmoded articles and implements of the kind that would
not even have found buyers at a church fête.

Trapp had cleared a floor area large enough to accommodate a canvas approximately six feet by ten feet wide. The
subject and artistic merit of the painting before him would
hardly have justified even its removal from the upright
position against the cellar wall where Trapp had discovered
it two months before. A charitable critic might have described
the rural scene it depicted as 'after Constable', meaning that
it was a long way behind the work of that English genius in
terms of style and execution. If the artist had lacked ability
she (for the picture was signed 'Ella Clare Symington,
1862') had not been wanting in courage. The canvas was
large, and it was filled. It was also true to say that, following
an exhaustive examination of everything contained in the
cellar, the picture was the only object Trapp had considered
worthy of further attention.

A similar search in the attic of his previous vicarage had
brought to light two flower-enamelled chamber pots, later
incontestably proved to be early Victorian. Trapp had
found a ready market for these at a price of forty pounds, a
sum he had forwarded, he thought appropriately, to the
Distressed Gentlefolks Aid Association. Nothing so immediately marketable had been revealed in the cellar at
Mitchell Stoke, and Trapp was not so ingenuous as to
believe that age of itself would invest the unframed painting
before him with any value that would not be cancelled by its

near hideous appearance. He was aware, however, that artists' materials were expensive and that a clean canvas of such dimensions might bring a reasonable price. Indeed, he had been assured of this fact by the young lady at the arts and crafts shop in Exeter, where he had gone for advice the day before. Now he was beginning what he assumed would be the comparatively simple job of cleaning off the paint with white spirit and cloth. The half-hour he had in hand before Maggie Edwards's funeral was time enough to make a start at least on one corner of the canvas to see if the process worked.

As he began his labour he resolved that the proceeds from the sale of the cleaned canvas should be donated to the Clergy Widows' Fund. He had earlier established that Ella Clare Symington had been the wife of Harold Clifton Symington, Vicar of St John's, Mitchell Stoke, from 1861 to 1907. He mused also on the propriety of suggesting to the Secretary of the Clergy Widows' Fund that art lessons might be included amongst the benefits dispensed.

CHAPTER V

Lunch at the Dower House was frugal in content and short in duration. Moonlight himself was withdrawn and pre-occupied. He was evidently not disposed to discuss re-acquiring Mitchell Hall in the presence of his wife, and Treasure, like every good banker, assumed he had been treated to a confidence although he had not been specifically cautioned on the point. True, he found it curious that Elizabeth might not yet be party to a proposition which so largely affected her. He engaged Elizabeth in general conversation for the short period they were all together in the dining-room, but he felt an unaccustomed relief when the meal was over.

The Moonlight household was one in which both host and hostess left guests to fend for themselves between meal-

times. Treasure found this an admirably civilized habit,
and particularly welcome in the circumstances. He intended
wasting no time in following up the promise he had made to
Moonlight.

Giving every appearance of being a gentleman engaged
on a post-prandial stroll, Treasure directed his steps from
the Dower House towards the Hall, crossing the gravelled
area that marked the way between the two houses on their
southern sides. In view of Timothy Trapp's experience
earlier in the day he was conscious that he risked being treated
as a trespasser – forewarned, even though he had abjured the
precaution of being forearmed.

As Treasure drew level with the main building of the
Hall the point Moonlight had made about the slope of the
ground became clear. The church itself, though appearing
to be set on high ground when viewed from the road, was
in fact a good deal less elevated than the Hall.

Although it was only a little after two o'clock, the army
of Filipinos was busily employed about its allotted task,
evidence that Scarbuck was not given to including lengthy
lunch-breaks in his packaged tours. Treasure was relieved to
observe that his approach – or perhaps the manner of his
coming – had not given rise to the kind of excitement that
had punctuated the Vicar's sudden appearance over the
wall. He noted, however, that his progress was being marked
by the overalled overseer of the work force. If challenged,
Treasure had already made up his mind to express innocent
surprise about his lack of right to reach the church by the
way he had chosen. He stopped as he drew near the earth-
works both to offer earnest of his intention by his demeanour
and to gratify a genuine interest. As he expected, this prompted a reaction from the overseer who came towards him, not
with indecent haste, but with the purposeful aim of a park
keeper about to admonish someone for not keeping off the
grass. The man's gait was unusual in a way that was not
entirely accounted for by his cumbersome attire. He seemed
to be leaning backwards as he walked, and his arms which he
swung from the elbows were not in exact rhythm with his

legs – like some raw and unsuitable recruit on an army parade ground.

'Excuse me, but this is private property, you know.' The voice was heavily affected, and following this opening pronouncement the speaker's whole body was momentarily contorted by a nervous wiggle, culminating in a toss of the head. The performance so far would have been described by Treasure's actress wife as distinctly 'camp'. The speaker looked to be in his late thirties. His complexion was pale, and his features gaunt. His wiry hair was close cropped at the sides, leaving a mane like the bristles of a scrubbing brush in the centre.

'I do beg your pardon,' said Treasure, 'I'm afraid I'm here by force of habit. Thoughtless of me to forget there's a new owner in residence. My name is Mark Treasure, by the way. I'm staying with my cousins the Moonlights.' He proffered his hand.

'Oh,' said the other, visibly mellowing as the two shook hands, 'well, I don't suppose Mr Scarbuck would mind really, it's just that I have my orders. I'm Eustace Dankton.'

'Not *the* Eustace Dankton?' replied Treasure, registering a surprise he did not in the least feel.

'Well, I suppose so,' Dankton almost purred. 'I mean I don't think there's another one.' This he followed with a demure toss of the head.

'Of course, I know you well by reputation,' lied Treasure, continuing quickly before he could be quizzed on this almost entirely unsupported statement. 'I suppose Mr Scarbuck has invited you here to keep an eye open for historical revelations while this kind of work is going on.' He nodded towards the excavation.

The hapless Dankton looked anything but the noted expert 'invited' to maintain a scholarly watchfulness over the proceedings, but he was only too ready to act the role he had just been credited despite appearances. 'Well that's exactly why I'm here,' he said in a tone that was almost confidential, 'but really I have to behave more like a works foreman with these little foreign busies hacking about at will;

you can't take your eye off them for a minute. I must look an absolute mess in this rig; too degrading really, but Mr Scarbuck insists *they* – ' waving an arm in the general direction of the 'foreign busies' – 'only recognize authority in uniform.'

'You look very appropriately dressed for a mucky job,' said Treasure encouragingly, taking a pace backward the better to admire Dankton's ridiculous appearance. 'Tell me, have you unearthed anything of interest?'

'Not a bloody thing. We've got the foundations of the pavilion that once stood here, of course.'

'I can see that,' observed Treasure, 'and it appears to have had a cellar. Wouldn't that have been unusual? I know the house well, and I don't recall there being a cellar beneath the eastern pavilion.'

'Oh, you never know with these places. This pavilion, or rather the one that used to be here, was probably a picture gallery. A cellar underneath could have had several uses . . . apart from keeping out the damp.'

Treasure moved nearer the workings, and after some slight hesitancy his companion fell in beside him. They stopped just short of the gaping hole. 'I see you have this side covered over,' said Treasure, indicating the huge tarpaulin draped down the left-hand wall of the deep rectangle.

'That's just to protect the er . . . the drain they're cutting for the swimming pool,' Dankton said uncertainly, 'in case of rain. Really I know nothing about the technicalities. Heavens above, I'm an antiquarian not a plumber.' This last protest appeared to be addressed not so much to Treasure as to the world at large, and with some feeling.

'Absolutely right, Eustace,' said a voice behind them. It was Scarbuck who had come upon them unseen around the vast mound of earth that had covered his arrival from the house, 'but we'll make a gaffer of you yet.' He eyed Treasure keenly. 'Mr Mark Treasure, if I'm not mistaken?'

'Quite right,' replied Treasure, bowing slightly, 'but how . . .'

'Oh come, Mr Treasure, I read the *Financial Times*, you know. They print your picture often enough, and I've watched you discussing money matters on the television. I thought it was you I saw arriving as I was leaving the Dower House this morning. Nice people, the Moonlights. There's quality there; blood will out no matter what they say.'

Treasure accepted this tribute to his kinsmen without demur. 'Yes, and it's strange to think of them as no longer the owners of this lovely house.'

'Ah, times and circumstances change, Mr Treasure. But better have me here who'll look after it than have the place fall down.'

Before Treasure could follow up a remark volunteered in precisely the direction he wanted the conversation to take, all three men were distracted by the sounds of a powerful, diesel-engined vehicle drawing up at the entrance to Mitchell Hall.

'That'll be the coach with all the lads,' cried Scarbuck, straightening his multicoloured headgear and brushing both his shoulders to ensure that no speck of dandruff further besmirched the national standard his jacket already so sadly defaced. 'All the regional leaders of Forward Britain; many prominent men amongst them, Mr Treasure. You'll no doubt know some of them – Griffith Speke-Jones MP for one.' And as though that probably exhausted the list of those members celebrated enough actually to be recognized: 'Come along with me, Mr Treasure, and say hello.'

The invitation was pointedly addressed to Treasure and not to Dankton, a fact which the latter accepted resignedly, remaining where he was standing as his employer drew Treasure away towards the side of the Hall. 'They're a grand bunch; patriots to a man. They're here for a day's relaxation – dinner tonight at the Hall and a round of golf in the morning. Most will be staying at The Bell, but I've got rooms ready for the top brass here in the house – no denigration intended of course, just not enough beds at the moment. Happen a few will be happier staying in a hotel in any case.'

As the two rounded the corner of the Hall the party of patriots was disgorging from the motor-coach. Most of the members bore the slightly dazed look common to those in polyglot parties of tourists thrown together on sightseeing tours of stately homes with nothing more in common than a shared conveyance. There was none of the hearty camaraderie that Treasure had expected. On the contrary, there was little conversation between members of the party arranging rather than assembling itself in the drive. There were some thirty persons in all; some stood alone, others formed small groups evidently in accordance with social standing. Treasure quickly noted this last point. Forward Britain clearly encompassed all classes of people amongst its leaders, but just as obviously failed to integrate them. One small group looked, to a man, the superannuated product of Sandhurst fallen on hard times – the bearing upright, the clothing good but weathered. Another group, much younger but far less at ease, Treasure assessed as middle management over-dressed, for safety, in business suits, and now regretting the caution in the context of the surroundings.

The largest and most animated group, clothed uniformly in dark blazers and grey trousers, could have been mistaken for half a touring cricket team. Treasure had no difficulty placing these since he recognized one of their number as a particularly arrogant young trade union official whose achievements in terms of personal publicity via the television screen seemed somehow not to be matched by his relative unimportance, or lack of matching progress, in his chosen calling. Then there was Griffith Speke-Jones.

As Scarbuck had expected, Treasure certainly recognized the one member of the party with a national reputation. The origins of Mr Speke-Jones were obscure and, apart from the studied maintenance of a marked Welsh accent, he had done his best to ensure that they remained so. In fact he had been the second son of a minor bank official in the Rhondda Valley. With the aid of scholarships and grants – plus a good deal of parental sacrifice – he had graduated through a lesser public school and a provincial university to a political career at a fairly early age – achieved and maintained more by guile than through any ideological commitment.

Speke-Jones had virtually made a profession of being all things to all men. His vulnerable position on the extreme right of the Labour Party was sustained only by a loyalty born of undeserved respect on the part of a sufficient, but latterly diminishing, number of constituents in a south-east London borough. These people, to a man – and woman, indeed especially the women – accepted his vague but colourful references to an upbringing of extreme poverty in the South Wales of the Depression, and many would have sworn he had gone shoeless and threadbare to school, although he had never actually told them so. The voters who remained faithful to Speke-Jones did so from a sense of self-identifica-tion. After all, he was one like them, but risen from an under-privileged position and thus qualified to be a worthy repre-sentative of the working man. He owned no such respect in Wales, a country he avoided visiting, though privately admitting that it was a good place to be from. He maintained two motor-cars – a large Jaguar for normal use, and a red Morris Mini for trips to his constituency.

While paying occasional lip-service to the doctrinaire socialist policies of the Party he was supposed to be repre-senting, and always voting in the right lobby on major issues, Speke-Jones had usually to be summoned by pocket radio receiver to evening Divisions in the House, either from the private dining tables of his many wealthy patrons, or from their West End clubs, at least on those few occasions when he had not succeeded in getting himself 'paired'. He enjoyed a standard of living that was not afforded or reflected by the size of his parliamentary stipend. The real source of his substantial income was as difficult to verify as the stories circulated about the deprivations surrounding his early life – though at least one of Her Majesty's Tax Inspectors had been conscientiously applying himself to resolving the first conundrum for a number of years.

Treasure had found himself in the same company as

Speke-Jones on several occasions, mostly at public dinners. He would nevertheless have hesitated before owning personal acquaintance with the politician.

'I've no doubt you two know each other.' This was Scarbuck presenting Speke-Jones.

'Oh, very well indeed,' said Speke-Jones running to form. 'Lovely to have you with us,' he continued, introducing a second presumption, and one that Treasure decided to correct.

'How d'you do,' he said pointedly. 'I'm hardly with you, I'm afraid. I just happen to be staying with some cousins next door.'

'You mean you're not one of us – not yet anyway; not one of those chosen to lead Britain forward?' Speke-Jones spoke half jocularly but loud enough for the statement to be caught by those standing near. 'Well, never mind; time enough, I'm sure.'

'Excuse me, won't you?' put in Scarbuck before Treasure had the opportunity to reply. 'A word of welcome.' He hurried to the top of the steps leading to the main door of Mitchell Hall. 'Friends,' he cried from this commanding position, arms outstretched to indicate that this salutation included all those within earshot.

Only the driver of the motor-coach engaged in unloading golf-bags from the boot of his vehicle chose modestly to exclude himself from this amicable verbal embrace. The others drew nearer the speaker in the first demonstration of solidarity since their arrival. Treasure decided to linger for a moment at the rear of the group.

CHAPTER VI

'Friends,' Scarbuck repeated, 'and if we aren't that, what are we . . .'

Judging from the furtive, sidelong glances produced by this rhetorical question, Treasure wondered whether he was the only one present who, if pressed, might have volunteered a discouraging reply.

'Friends in advertency, comrades in the army of the right, crusaders in the cause . . .' Scarbuck consulted some notes . . .' in the cause of freeing this great nation from its shekels . . .' he looked closer at the notes . . .' its shekels. Welcome to Mitchell Hall where "King and Country" has been the rallying cry for centuries on end – "Queen and Country" it is now of course, but it's the sentiment that counts.'

This last impromptu tribute to women's rights produced involuntary murmers of 'hear, hear' from the Sandhurst set. The rest of the audience was unmoved.

'From now onwards these historic precincts will be the nerve-centre of our great movement,' Scarbuck continued. 'Some of you will rest tonight within its hospitable wards . . . er . . . walls. The others will be comfortably accommodated in a nearby hostelry, please see the instructions on your invitations.'

Those in the middle-management group, and to a man, dutifully unzipped the document cases they were carrying and produced pieces of paper which they then studiously examined as though for the first time.

'Today you're here for well-earned relaxation and recreation. Soon, though, Mitchell Hall will be converted into a place for study and instruction, a national centre for pilgrims ready to become apostles.' Scarbuck paused, searching his notes for more material, but finding none continued uncertainly. 'I'm not making a speech to you now, that'll come after dinner . . .'

There was an audible groan from the leader of the trade union contingent.

'These few . . . er . . . kind words are just to make you feel at home before they take you away . . . that is, before the coach takes some of you on to The Bell . . .'

'Scarbuck and I are playing nine holes at four o'clock. We'd be delighted to have you join us.' Speke-Jones was at Treasure's side.

The banker hesitated before replying. Golf with two such

undesirables had hardly featured in his weekend plans. Yet the need for a private word with Scarbuck about the ownership of Mitchell Hall was urgent. If the man was to be surrounded by 'apostles' until the following day, then opportunities would be limited.

'That would suit me very well,' said Treasure truthfully. 'Shall we say four o'clock on the tee? And now I really must be off – sorry to miss the end of Scarbuck's stirring oration.'

'Comic turn more like,' said Speke-Jones with undisguised contempt.

Treasure made off down the drive toward the main gate of Mitchell Hall. He had decided to walk to the churchyard by the road to avoid another confrontation with Dankton. It was already two-thirty – the time he had arranged to meet Thelma Goodbody. The fact he was hurrying as he turned into the road might have made the collision inevitable with the figure coming in the opposite direction. But the man made no apology, and what was more, he stood his ground after the abrupt encounter, effectively barring Treasure's way. He was young, and self-consciously muscular; his hair was blond and curly, his skin unseasonably bronzed; he wore a tight-fitting blue denim suit, a pink, open-necked shirt, and an assortment of jewellery that Treasure found as distinctly un-masculine as the floral scent that wafted downwind from the man's direction.

'Now get this clear and get it straight. Stacey and I want more out of this than you're giving, and I'm the one with the guts and the muscle to do something about it. The deal is fifty-fifty or you're a dead man, and it won't be an accident like this morning. And don't try turning your pygmies on to me either. I'm around and I'm staying around – and not just to do the dirty work for no thanks.' Having delivered this incredible statement, the man strode across the road to a yellow Volkswagen. He next drove away at high speed in the direction of the church, leaving a dumbfounded Treasure staring after him.

One thing was certain; Treasure had been mistaken for

someone else. The most likely candidate was Scarbuck in
view of the obvious reference to the Filipinos. But who was
the accident victim of that morning – Treasure had heard of
no accident – and what was the nature of 'the deal' that the
blond man and 'Stacey' (his wife? – girl-friend? – partner in
crime?) were doing with the new owner of Mitchell Hall?

If Scarbuck had really been the intended object of the
stranger's verbal assault then the hatred evident in the man's
tone and manner certainly equalled that expressed in more
civilized terms by Moonlight that morning. Remembering
the contempt that Speke-Jones had shown for Scarbuck a few
minutes earlier, and the smouldering distaste exhibited for
that same personage by Dankton, Treasure concluded that
Scarbuck was a figure singularly lacking in friends. Treasure
was sufficiently versed in current idiom not to assess the
statement 'you're a dead man' as an actual threat to life, but
the way in which the words had been uttered certainly
predicated seriously unpleasant consequences – and the
speaker had possessed all the physical and mental attributes
of a promisingly violent disposition.

Treasure quickened his pace towards the church as the
little yellow car noisily spun around the corner and out of
sight, its colour and speed contrasting with the sombre, still
group of vehicles and men grouped around the little lych-
gate of the church. A number of cars were parked alongside
the low wall that skirted the road, headed by a hearse.
Maggie Edwards's funeral was in progress inside the church
and the drivers of the hearse and two attendant black limou-
sines, looking professionally morose in black top-coats and
bowler hats, were standing beside the second car smoking
to fill in the time, but doing so in a fashion that gave an
appearance appropriately mournful.

Miss Goodbody was waiting patiently for Treasure just
inside the gate. 'Have you heard of an accident today?' was
Treasure's unexpected greeting.

'No, but if that maniac in the yellow Volkswagen stays
loose much longer there'll be one,' the girl replied spiritedly.
'I'm sure it was the same car that nearly ran into us this

morning on the way here.'

'I thought it was vaguely familiar.' Treasure decided not
to volunteer a commentary on the driver.

'What do you think?' Miss Goodbody had a more pressing
subject for discussion than dangerous drivers. 'The gravedigger's absolutely disappeared – left poor Timothy completely in the lurch.'

'Did he leave a note?' asked Treasure lightly.

'Nothing so thoughtful, I'm afraid. He's just done a bunk.
Timothy was in a terrible tizz. Fortunately the grave's dug,
but it'll need filling in shortly. We've managed to recruit
Mr Banquet – the husband of Timothy's housekeeper – but
he's not a bit pleased about it. He usually takes Saturday
afternoons off to watch football in Reading.'

The two walked together towards the north porch of the
church. The building was larger than one would expect in
a village the size of Mitchell Stoke, but it had self-evidently
not been built of a piece at one time. The apsidal east end
was Norman and heavily buttressed. The much higher nave
was Early English and boasted a clerestory. Another genera-
tion, perhaps not wishing to appear lowlier and less pious
than its predecessors, had added a squat tower, but in brick,
not stone like the rest of the church. Even so, as if to make
amends, this Elizabethan addition incorporated a nave
extension with a very fine west window, delicately traced.
As in so many other similar cases the total effect was har-
monious – just as a succession of careful masons had intended
it should be despite the mixture of styles and materials.
Even a mid-Victorian southern aisle only visible from the
vicarage approach to the Church had been fashioned with
more sensitivity than was common amongst Gothic revivalists.

Treasure enjoyed the church without needing to dissect
its parts. It was an old familiar which he found somehow
comforting for that, even though his taste in architecture was
firmly classical and not romantic. While obliged to admit
that he had been brought up 'perpendicular', he was given
to protesting that he had come of age a Renaissance man.

The path the two were following bisected just before the

church porch. One part continued on to the church while
the other branched left running parallel with the nave and
rounding the east end. There it converged with the path
from the vicarage garden, thereafter running eastwards
through the churchyard and terminating at the gateway
surmounted by Trapp that morning.

Just beyond where the paths converged stood the Acropolis, the monument to the first baronet. It was a miniature
imitation of the upper portion of a Roman temple-tomb.
Thus its local name was hardly appropriate, owing its
origin more to the fact that the edifice was elevated than
the suggestion that it pre-dated Greek Revival by a hundred
years.

Fashioned to resemble the frame of an open, square
temple, instead of surmounting a classically conventional
raised tomb, the building sat on a three-stepped podium which
set it two feet above ground level. To the irreverent, the
whole resembled nothing so much as a small stone bandstand.
Each of its faces was topped by a plain pediment. The roof
was supported at the corners by square Tuscan pillars
punctuating the lines of free-standing columns that formed
tetrastyle colonnades on all four sides.

'And would you believe it – architect unknown,' exclaimed
Treasure as he and Miss Goodbody ascended the steps to
stand in the centre of the flat stone floor.

'Very nice,' volunteered Miss Goodbody politely.

'Very nice!' Treasure exploded in mock horror. 'Here
you are, standing inside a probably unique and certainly
powerfully significant architectural gem, and all you can
say is "very nice". Look at the symmetry. The base is
fifteen feet square – I know because I measured the whole
thing years ago – and everything else is in perfect classical
proportion. Whoever put this together was a scholar and a
perfectionist – probably spent months sketching and
measuring in Italy and had the wit to be more impressed
with Greek copies there than with Roman originals. He
even put entasis into the columns – you can see if you stand
outside.' Miss Goodbody looked uncertain. 'And you can

look up entasis as a penance for saying "very nice".'

'And the tomb's underneath?' asked the girl in as humble a tone as she could muster.

'No, there's no tomb. The old man was buried in the church before this was built. You're quite right, though, in assuming there ought to be,' Treasure added patronizingly. 'The Greeks and Romans would have had a roomy square tomb under this floor, raising the whole thing a third as much again off the ground. This is just a cenotaph, but the floor foundations probably go down several feet – there's not a sign of subsidence or cracking anywhere; nothing quite like it at the time in England.'

'Or in Greece and Italy either by the sound of it.' Miss Goodbody was daring to retaliate.

Treasure smiled. 'Point to you. True, it's not a replica, just an intelligent, sensitive application of principles. I wish we knew who'd done it. I've always imagined it was some enthusiastic amateur, a friend of the second baronet's fresh from the Grand Tour and longing to build something . . . anything, and Moonlight, wanting a memorial to his father, gave the chap a chance. Probably he never built another thing or else the creator of this would be known.'

'All right – it's jolly good,' said Miss Goodbody, 'but to be honest I'm more interested in the man it commemo-rates – he very likely walked and talked with Shakespeare.'

'And on this very spot,' commented Treasure, humouring the whim. 'According to Arthur Moonlight, all the area beyond was occupied by the old monastery building until the mid-sixteen-thirties.' The two looked eastward across the rising, undulating ground that led up to the wall. It was a patchwork of mounds and furrows, dotted by occasional gravestones mostly at drunken angles.

Absently, Treasure noted again the single, symmetrical feature in what was otherwise a hotchpotch landscape. A few yards to the east of where they were standing was an elevated, stone-sided grave, and mid-way between this and the wall was another such, virtually identical to the first. The two made a straight line with the Acropolis pointing back to the church. Miss Goodbody followed Treasure's gaze, then walked across to the first of the tombs.

'Why would a grave have an iron grille?' she asked, running her hand along a foot-wide metal trellis that ran the length of the tomb just below its flat stone top.

'For decoration, probably,' answered Treasure, joining her. The grille appeared on all four sides, interrupted only by stone supports at the corners. 'These two tombs have always intrigued me,' the banker continued, indicating the matching tomb further along the path. 'Possibly the gent buried here was an iron mason and he, or his family, wanted posterity to be aware of the fact. The idea worked too; look, the inscription's weathered away but the iron's still good, if a bit rusty.'

'And his brother's over here?' called Miss Goodbody who was moving on toward the other grave. 'The two are practically identical.'

Treasure was too preoccupied to comment. He had made a find of his own which gave him a feeling of inexplicable unease. The iron grille he had grasped on the first tomb, and on the side facing the Acropolis, had moved under his hand. It had not come away, for it was slotted in a fashion that held it in place from the inside; but the grille had moved – an unexpected event in a component part of a small edifice that had weathered perhaps three hundred and fifty years intact. Treasure walked around the tomb testing the other three grilles. Not only was each immovable but also effectively sealed at the edges with heavy growths of moss. While some moss adhered to the edges of the grille Treasure had first examined, this framing was not complete. He sought and found lengths of moss which might recently have formed part of the grille's surround scattered on the ground beside the tomb.

'The funeral's coming.' Miss Goodbody was at Treasure's elbow. 'D'you think we should decently retire?' A solemn, small procession was emerging from the church door. Treasure nodded in agreement and motioned Miss Goodbody towards the south side of the churchyard in the general

direction of an immense Victorian sarcophagus that promised
them shelter from observation by the mourners approaching
in the middle distance. They were not alone in this stratagem.
As they rounded the tomb they came upon one whom Treasure rightly assumed to be Mr Banquet, taking his ease,
until called for duty, on a south-facing step, with a cigarette
and a copy of the *Sun*.

Despite the warmth of the afternoon Mr Banquet appeared
to be cocooned in layers of ancient woollen jerseys, his head
enclosed in a khaki, knitted Balaclava, topped by a tweed
cap of good quality but fallen on hard times since – or
possibly before – being handed down to Mr Banquet by one
of his affluent employers. What could be seen of his features
gave Mr Banquet the appearance of an over-fed mole.

'This ain't right, miss.' He was addressing Miss Goodbody though he had already acknowledged Treasure's
presence with a glare.

'But, Mr Banquet, the Vicar did agree three pounds,'
the girl said anxiously. Banquet sighed and then seemed
earnestly to contemplate the large shovel at his side. It
was to this implement that he addressed his next remark.

'It's not that; it's 'Orace.' He glanced at Treasure. ''Im
that's disappeared. He wouldn't 'ave done it, see, not with
a job on, not 'Orace.' Following this fine testimonial to the
conscientious habit of Mr Worple, Banquet returned to
an examination of his shovel, at the same time deliberately
folding up his newspaper and stuffing it into the belt exposed
momentarily under layers of woollen garments.

'You're concerned about the well-being of the gravedigger,' translated Treasure. The mole-like eyes surveyed
the speaker.

'Not 'is well-being; more like 'is ill-being to my way of
thinking.' The tone was ominous.

'No accident has been reported?' enquired Treasure,
mindful of his encounter earlier with the driver of the yellow
car.

'Don't mean to say 'e 'asn't 'ad one. Tin' bleedin' natural,
not at all it in't.'

CHAPTER VII

Having established that Banquet intended to carry through his contract to fill in the grave, Miss Goodbody was showing a decided lack of interest in the conversation. She pointedly addressed Treasure. 'I've promised to help Timothy clean a canvas after the funeral. I could show you the parish register I was telling you about if you'd like to come over to the vicarage now – and there are some parish council minute books we haven't been through yet,' she offered as further inducement.

Treasure glanced at his watch. 'I've got a golf date at four, but why don't we wander off anyway, the funeral should be over in a minute or two.' He turned to offer some parting pleasantry to Banquet but the latter was wholly engaged, removing his boots for a purpose Treasure judged was connected with the task of grave-filling that shortly lay before him. He noted that Banquet was wearing two pairs of socks that were only odd in the sense that each matching pair adorned one foot.

As Treasure and Miss Goodbody approached the vicarage through the gate that led there directly from the churchyard, a small Panda police car swung into the drive and stopped before the front door. A uniformed policeman alighted and disappeared from view into the porch.

'Good afternoon, Officer,' said Treasure as he and his companion approached the young man waiting lawfully before the wide-open door, but under the baleful gaze of the recumbent Bach who lay semi-somnolent in the hall.

'That bell doesn't work,' volunteered Miss Goodbody, 'and neither does the watch-dog apparently. The Vicar's in the churchyard finishing a funeral. Can we help?'

'Afternoon, sir,' replied the policeman, saluting smartly. 'Constable Humble, Thames Valley Police.' And proud and eager at the fact, was Treasure's approving conclusion.

Humble turned to Miss Goodbody. 'I'm not sure, miss. We've just had a call from headquarters.' He paused and Treasure envisioned the strings of heavily manned police posts charged to contact Officer Humble at all costs.

'Regarding a Mr Horace Worple? There's been an accident?' Treasure's words came more as a statement than an enquiry.

'Yes, sir, that's right, sir.' Humble hesitated, evidently concerned not to exceed his brief. Treasure straightened and consciously attempted to look as much like a member of the ruling class as was possible.

'Is the man dead?' Both Humble and Miss Goodbody looked at him in surprise.

'As a matter of fact he is, sir,' replied Humble producing a note-book and pencil. 'Might I have your name, sir?'

'I'm Mark Treasure and this is Miss Thelma Goodbody. Would you like to borrow this?' He proffered a gold Cross ball-pen; Constable Humble had broken his pencil. 'I'm staying at Mitchell Hall with Arthur Moonlight.'

'With Sir Arthur, sir.' Humble appeared both impressed and relieved.

'Yes. Tell me, was Mr Worple's death an accident?'

The constable swallowed. 'Not exactly, sir, that is we're not sure of the cause of death. CID are on to it, though.' Another pause, then with evident relief Humble's gaze moved over Treasure's shoulder and he called, 'Afternoon, Vicar.'

'Hello, Vincent.' Trapp joined the group, and stood rocking on his heels. 'How's your mother?'

Constable Humble looked slightly embarrassed at this parochial enquiry. 'Much better, Vicar. Should be in church tomorrow.' Trapp beamed. 'I'm here on official business, Vicar.' Humble did his best to look official, unaided by the juvenating outcrop of pimples on his chin. He recounted the information he had already given to Treasure and Miss Goodbody. 'And they told me at the church, Vicar, that you saw Mr Worple this morning.'

'Yes, I did, around ten-thirty,' said Trapp. 'Tell me,

where did you find Worple?'

'I didn't find him, Vicar, it was Windsor Police . . .' He paused, looking from Trapp to Treasure and Miss Goodbody, and back again.

'Come on, Vincent, out with it, these people are trusted friends, and we shan't tell anyone if it's an official secret.'

Treasure nearly protested that it very probably was, and that it was unfair to press this obviously inexperienced young policeman to divulge more than he had done already. Then his curiosity got the better of him.

'Well,' said Humble, reserve evaporated, youthful excitement replacing it, 'Mr Worple was found dead in a burning houseboat just below Old Windsor at noon today. His back was broken and there's thought to be knife wounds in his chest.' There was a pause while Humble gathered breath to give the right effect to his gravest announcement. 'Foul play is suspected.' Having delivered this blistering news, the young policeman bit his lower lip. 'And I'll be in awful trouble if you tell anyone, Vicar.'

Humble's afterthought had been offered none too soon. As he spoke, a grey Ford car drew up in the Vicarage drive. Its sole occupant, a tall, slim man in early middle age, was dressed in a brown sports jacket and grey flannel trousers. His dark hair was cut short, and he wore a fisherman's trilby hat adorned with sufficient coloured flies to offer proper earnest of its owner's genuine piscatorial involvement. As the man alighted from the car Constable Humble drew himself to attention and delivered a salute that would have done justice to a Colour Sergeant confronted by the Colonel of the Regiment.

The man nodded approvingly at Humble, and treated the other three to a broad smile, raising his hat in the direction of Miss Goodbody. 'Lovely afternoon,' he observed in a soft tone and accent that Treasure involuntarily placed as educated Oxfordshire yeoman. 'My name's Colin Bantree, your friendly neighbourhood Detective Chief Inspector, CID. Sorry to barge in like this, but as I expect you've

learned from Constable Humble, we've got a spot of bother.'
He beamed at the Vicar as if to signify that clergymen and
policemen, at least, were no strangers to bother of one kind
or another. 'Mr Trapp, I presume?' He held out his hand.
'Don't think we've met before. How's the new safe holding
out?'

It had been at the suggestion of the Thames Valley Police,
warmly supported by all members of the Parochial Church
Council, that a safe had recently been installed in the vestry
of St John's, Mitchell Stoke, to house those few remaining
church valuables that had survived the first few months of
Timothy Trapp's incumbency, plus some replacements
provided by a reluctant and admonishing insurance company.
The two keys supplied had been left in the keeping of the
Vicar's Warden and the People's Warden who, much to
Trapp's delight, had thereafter been obliged to attend, one
or other of them, every service held in the church. Since, with
the exception of Holy Communion, which he celebrated
daily, Trapp was not much in favour of the lengthier, statutory observances as laid down in the Book of Common
Prayer, he had already recruited the support of those two
important members of the parish in his aim considerably
to shorten the number and the length of such observances.
Thus, Trapp wholly approved of the safe for reasons entirely
unconnected with its function. 'It's an admirable safe,
thank you, Inspector,' he replied before introducing Treasure
and Miss Goodbody.

Constable Humble coughed loudly. 'Are you in urgent
need of medication, Humble,' enquired Chief Inspector
Bantree, smiling, 'or is that your way of discreetly attracting
my attention?'

'The latter, sir. Begging your pardon, sir, this gentleman – '
he indicated Treasure – 'is staying with Sir Arthur Moonlight,
sir.'

'Then I shall show him due deference, Humble, have no
fear of that.'

'No, sir, what I mean, sir, is that he indicated he might be
able to throw some light on the . . . er . . . crime, sir.'

'Nothing so useful, I'm afraid, Inspector,' Treasure interjected. 'Just before you arrived I offered the reasonable conjecture that Worple might have met with a fatal accident.'

'Reasonable conjecture, Mr Treasure?' The Inspector repeated the phrase slowly.

'Yes, reasonable in the sense that Worple appears to have been a conscientious sort of man. He had a job to do this afternoon and any accident that prevented him from sending word about his non-appearance would have needed to be a pretty serious one.'

Treasure appreciated that this explanation was less than perfect, and just as he already regretted his incautious comment to Humble, he had no intention of volunteering more information for the time being, and for his own reasons. He was nevertheless aware that as a good citizen he should take this instant opportunity to recount the story of his meeting with the driver of the yellow Volkswagen. Already there was little doubt in Treasure's mind that the man who had threatened him outside the gate of Mitchell Hall was in some way involved with the disappearance of Worple – if not with his death, accidental or otherwise. Even so, other events during the day prompted him to keep his own counsel until he could be sure that the curiously perturbed Arthur Moonlight was in no way involved. In mitigation the man had very firmly stated that he intended to remain in Mitchell Stoke and had indicated he had pressing reasons for doing so.

'The accident was certainly serious, Mr Treasure.' The Inspector appeared to be weighing his listener more than his words. 'We have reason to believe . . . sorry, one drops into the jargon so easily. We know that the late Mr Worple died of a broken back or of knife wounds, or a combination of both. What we don't know is where he died and how he came to be transported, presumably dead, to a private boat shed near Windsor, and deposited in a cabin cruiser which was subsequently set on fire.'

Constable Humble let out an audible sigh of relief.

'I understand you saw Mr Worple this morning, Vicar?'

'Yes, and spoke to him where he was working in the churchyard. That would have been at about ten . . . er . . . twenty. He seemed very well.' Trapp realized too late the limpness of this last remark, had Worple really been suffering from a broken back and stab wounds at the time of their encounter.

'Now that's a thoroughly useful bit of information,' said the Inspector encouragingly, referring presumably to the statement about time and not the one concerning the health of the deceased. 'I'll ask you later to be as exact as you can about the time you left Mr Worple; it may be critical. My guess is you may have been the last person – innocent person, that is – to see him alive.' Trapp was grateful for the qualification, but too soon. 'I imagine you'd have no difficulty establishing your whereabouts between ten-fifteen and, say, one o'clock today, Vicar?'

'None whatsoever, Inspector.'

'Good . . . Yes, well, as I say, you were probably the last person to speak to Mr Worple. He left his home – that's Arden Cottage' (Miss Goodbody looked up in surprise) 'just up the road, at eight-fifteen. He lives, or rather lived, with his married daughter and her husband. He was a widower. My sergeant's with the daughter now, we called there first.'

'Inspector – ' this was Treasure – 'may I ask how you came to identify the body so quickly? Windsor is some distance away . . .'

'Quite easily, sir. Mr Worple had an unposted football pool coupon in his pocket. It was filled in, complete with name and address. No postal order though, or stamp. I expect he was a bit short of money this week, aren't we all.' Bantree smiled at Trapp and Miss Goodbody before returning a more serious gaze at Treasure as if to indicate that he might be the only one present who was not currently feeling the pinch. 'There'll be the matter of formal identification, of course,' he continued, 'but I'm afraid there's no doubt. I viewed the body myself an hour ago and comparing it with photographs I've just been looking at in the cottage, it's

Mr Worple all right.'

'Was the fire a serious one?' Treasure asked.

'Fire? Did I mention a fire?' Treasure suspected he was being made to feel undeservedly guilty. He was getting the measure of Inspector Bantree's disarming technique.

'Yes, you did,' Trapp put in firmly.

'Of course I did.' Bantree smiled. 'Well now, there we were lucky. The owner of the boat-shed is away on some archaeological expedition abroad. If whoever put the body in there knew this, he might have assumed the place would have been deserted. In fact, quite by chance, the owner's son came down from London with his girl-friend to give the boat a spring clean – favour to the old man, I suppose. They must have missed our body-snatcher, or dumper, by minutes. If he started the fire – and we have to assume he did – he made a rotten job of it, and the young people put it out before the brigade arrived. Not much damage, and certainly none to the remains of Mr Worple.'

'The whole thing sounds a bit amateur,' said Trapp. 'I mean, if the idea was for Worple to disappear without trace, leaving identification on him was a bit daft.'

'I quite agree, Vicar. If the fire had taken a hold there wouldn't have been much left of the body, or the identification for that matter. Of course we'd have found out eventually who it was, but it might have taken some time. No, my first impression is that our . . . murderer . . . was in a tearing hurry, and that time was more important to him than eventual discovery of his victim or the chap's identity. Strange. There are certainly more permanent ways of getting rid of a body, but in daylight, and with no time to spare . . .'

'Do you know the name of the owner of the boat-house, Inspector?' asked Treasure in as casual a voice as he could manage.

'Yes, I've got it here somewhere,' Bantree fished in his pockets. 'Here it is. Canwath-Wright, a Colonel Canwath-Wright, ex-Royal Engineers I gather, and a big-wig in the archaeological world. Know him?' He looked at Treasure keenly.

'No,' said Treasure truthfully, and he was not in the least tempted to add that he knew someone who did.

Being excused further interlocution by Inspector Bantree, Treasure left the group but attempted not to display undue haste in the matter. The Inspector required further information from Trapp concerning the time and detail of his conversation with the ill-fated Worple, and as Treasure returned to the churchyard he was pleased to see, from a backward glance, that the party was disappearing into the vicarage. Thereafter, he made all speed to reach the Dower House for an urgent conversation with Moonlight.

Elizabeth Moonlight was arranging flowers in the hall. 'Arthur's gone into Oxford to hunt for something in Hertford College library.' She sighed. 'If he hadn't made that grand gesture and given so many books away we'd still have a proper reference library here – the saving in petrol would have been enormous.' She stood back, head on one side, assessing the pleasing results of her efforts with a handful of daffodils and a great deal more of greenery. 'Still,' she continued ruminatively, 'he enjoys his little chats with the odd don he runs into. I've always thought he'd have been happier teaching at a university than he was as a soldier. Though one never really knows.' She smiled at Treasure resignedly. 'Did you want him urgently – is it about this Scarbuck business?'

'How do you mean?' asked Treasure guardedly.

'Oh come on, Mark darling, my wits are not in total decline. Arthur wants the Hall back and he's using you as an intermediary.'

'Has he told you this?'

'No, he hasn't, but you don't live with a man for more than twenty years without twigging when he's bothered about something, and knowing when he's doing something about it. After he'd 'phoned you last night he was like a dog with two tails – and he'd been depressed most of the week. I knew he hadn't asked you down just because I love you so

much. I do all the same.' She gave Treasure a light kiss on
the cheek. 'Heaven knows why Arthur wants the Hall back,
though I think the unspeakable Scarbuck may be reason
enough. We're not all that well off, you know.' Treasure did
know, and more about the Moonlight family finances than
he suspected Elizabeth knew herself.

'Any idea when Arthur will be back?'

'Yes, he said six o'clock, and you know how pedantic he is
with timing. So if you want to ravish me before my husband
returns – ' Elizabeth glanced at her watch – 'you have exactly
two and a half hours. On second thoughts you'd better find
something else to do because I have the dinner to prepare –
so you can stop looking so worried!'

Treasure took both her hands in his. 'Elizabeth, this is
important. Were you and Arthur in the house all this
morning?'

She thought for a moment. 'Yes, we were.'

'Together?'

'Most of the time. We read the papers in the study
after breakfast . . . oh, and then I cleared off to the kitchen
because Scarbuck was coming by appointment at half
past ten. Actually, Timothy arrived with him.' She paused.
'Then you came. But why is it important?'

Treasure ignored the question. 'So neither you nor Arthur
were in the churchyard? You didn't see this fellow Worple?'

'No, we didn't. But you know Mr Worple's disappeared?
Has something happened to him?'

'He appears to have been murdered.'

CHAPTER VIII

Treasure decided to keep his appointment with Scarbuck
and Speke-Jones at four o'clock. He had told Elizabeth
Moonlight all he had learned about the fate of Horace
Worple – information which, despite her planned domestic
programme, had sent her hurrying round to Arden Cottage

with words of comfort for Worple's married daughter. The Worples were 'old village'.

Arthur Moonlight would certainly not return before the hour he had stated. Treasure knew and enjoined his classically firm attitude to the ordering and allocation of time. In the circumstances Treasure would have no opportunity before six o'clock to discuss with his friend the various aspects of the day's discoveries and events that disturbed him – chiefly on Moonlight's account. Equally, he was now more than ever determined to progress his commission to beard Scarbuck on the subject of selling Mitchell Hall during the game.

Treasure had driven the half mile to the Mid-Stoke Golf Club in the Rolls. The Club House was half this distance approached on foot from the Moonlights' garden, the boundary of which marched with part of the eighteenth fairway. Treasure nevertheless took the car, reflecting – as would many golfers in the same circumstances – that walking to a golf-course was an inexplicably unacceptable chore in contrast to the pleasure of walking on a golf-course, ball in play.

Treasure was a 'country member' of Mid-Stoke, despite the fact that his home was in Cheyne Walk, Chelsea. This did not suggest that the Club Secretary was peculiarly ill-informed about the shortage of green fields in the South West London postal districts. The Club rules specified simply that any member living more than forty miles from the course was entitled to pay a reduced subscription. Membership of Mid-Stoke at any price was something of an extravagance for Treasure since he seldom played there. Even so, Moonlight was Life President of the Club, and having been made a founder member, initially at Moonlight's expense, Treasure had always felt that to resign might have appeared disloyal.

Mid-Stoke is not a challenging course. Laid out in 1948 on a limited budget, its composition had been governed, more than anything, by the need to create saleable house-building sites at strategic points along its length. The resulting architectural atmosphere of the course was Norman Shaw traditional, and bland to the point of boredom. Nevertheless, since most of the residents and members qualified for a similar description, in a sense, horses had been found for courses – although, in this instance, there was only one course.

The Club House, a Lutyens-sized version of the houses nearby, was sufficiently close to both the ninth and the eighteenth greens to make taking one's ease upon its substantial terrace a hazardous pastime. Golf-balls tended to land, full toss, amongst the tables or upon the members seated there without warning, though so far without fatality. The building's situation did, however, offer compensation in the sense that both the first and the tenth tee lay close by. Thus, those members who wished to play only nine holes were at liberty to do so without the inconvenience of finding themselves in open country at the finish. Although half a game of golf provides only proportional satisfaction to most golfers, an hour and a half of recreation is often better than no recreation at all.

It was not this last thought that Treasure had in mind as he stood, practising his swing, on the first tee. The time was ten minutes after four and the half-hour safety margin he had earlier estimated he had in hand to play the game and return to the Dower House before Arthur Moonlight was fast reducing. It was with some relief, then, that as he looked up from his watch he observed Scarbuck and his party rounding the side of the Club House. The sight also appealed at once to his sense of comedy.

To Treasure's immense relief, Scarbuck had forsaken all the bizarre garments he had been wearing earlier, save for the cap. He was now dressed in a white polo-necked sweater, blue plus-fours and red stockings over blue golf shoes. He succeeded in looking no less conspicuous than he had earlier, but somehow the red, white and blue combination was less embarrassingly obtrusive. He was followed by a diminutive Filipino with a worried expression, and an immense golf bag which seemed to dwarf its bearer. Close behind came Speke-Jones, pulling a golf trolley. The politician, like Treasure, was casually but properly attired for golf.

'We're all ready then,' said Scarbuck heartily and in place of the apology that Treasure had been expecting. 'I'd have brought you a caddy if I'd thought. I call this one Fred – that's not his real name, but he doesn't speak English and I don't speak Filipino so what's the difference? The Vicar crocked him this morning, but he'll do for carrying a bag.'

'I can manage thank you.' Treasure nodded at Speke-Jones. 'Shall we make a start? I'm playing off six.'

'Twenty-four,' said Scarbuck, as though proud of possessing the highest permitted handicap in golf.

'Six is almost vulgarly good,' put in Speke-Jones. 'No doubt the product of a well-spent youth, Mr Treasure,' he added in a tone that implied he meant the opposite of what he said. 'I'm eighteen, but you can't be good at everything! So you give us both strokes. Big money game, is it?'

'I should find 10p for the winner a sufficient incentive,' replied the vice-chairman of one of Britain's most affluent merchant banks.

'Done,' said Scarbuck. 'Well, age before beauty,' he continued, placing a ball on the tee. Fred arranged himself and the enormous bag immediately in front of his employer. 'Nay, lad, that's not the place. Come over here.'

Scarbuck grasped his caddy by the shoulders and propelled him to the side of the tee. 'That's . . . where . . . you . . . stand,' he said, slowly and deliberately as though this would overcome Fred's total inability to translate the words addressed to him. 'Now . . . don't . . . move.' He pressed down hard on the little man's shoulders.

Scarbuck returned to address the ball, or more accurately to give the impression that he was about to hammer it into the ground with a short downward stroke from the wooden clubhead he held hovering six inches above its gleaming white cover. The hovering went on for some moments accompanied by heavy breathing from Scarbuck. At the point when Treasure was beginning to find the suspense unnerving, some unseen force seemed to impel the clubhead heavenwards at incredible speed. Momentarily, Treasure imagined that the club, with Scarbuck in tow, was being lifted into the sky in the manner depicted in so many *Punch* cartoons portraying old gentlemen attached to umbrellas in howling gales. A fraction of a second before the fully extended Scarbuck might have been expected actually to levitate – only his toes remained in contact with the earth – the clubhead came downwards with the same speed that it had gone upwards, its wielder now appearing to collapse under the pressure of some crushing power exerted on his person from above.

There was a shower of grass and earth uplifted from the area immediately behind the ball, accompanied by an unwholesome 'ping' as the rounded toe of the club came into violent contact with the hard, white sphere, propelling it with tremendous force in the immediate direction of the well-anchored caddy. 'Ow!' screamed little Fred, an expression that would have gained nothing in translation. He crumpled in a heap upon the ground, grasping a part of his anatomy well below the belt and too sensitive and pained for even elementary decorum to prevail against the reflex application of aid.

Fred, his whole body contorted into an uneven ball, rolled about on the ground like some professional footballer grievously fouled for the second time in full view of the television cameras. He screamed and screeched and then began to weep copiously. Scarbuck hurried across from the tee. 'Did it hit him?' he enquired lamely, and in the circumstances unnecessarily. 'Undo your trousers, lad,' he continued, attempting to take hold of the writhing Filipino by the leather belt that encircled his middle.

Scarbuck's fumbling produced an unexpected reaction. His caddy, already severely wounded, albeit by remote control but for all he knew by the malicious, considered action of the man who had so firmly placed him in the line of fire, now concluded that the same oppressor was about to inflict yet more tortures upon his person. Leaping to his feet, head bent in the manner of a battering ram, he charged Scarbuck in the stomach with a force that toppled the older man, then sent him sinking to the ground. Fred next started to run, and despite a lop-sided gait, made good speed in the general direction of the Club House, leaving the colourful, collapsed Scarbuck looking like Humpty Dumpty.

'I'll murder that little heathen when I get hold of him,' Scarbuck exploded.

'Well, better make certain he doesn't get hold of you first,' said Speke-Jones who, with Treasure, was helping Scarbuck to his feet. 'He might bear a little grudge after what you just did to him; never know with Orientals – isn't that right, Mr Treasure?' and without waiting for a reply he went on, 'Didn't you say the Vicar knocked him about already today?'

'Yes, and a pity he didn't break his neck.' Scarbuck was still ruffled. He brushed himself down and glanced at his golf bag lying where it had been abandoned on the ground.

'Looks as though you've been left to carry the white man's burden, George,' said Speke-Jones lightly. 'Tell you what, I'll carry my bag and you can put yours on my trolley.'

'No, thanks,' Scarbuck replied, rubbing his stomach, 'quite put me off my game, that has.' A comment that produced a shrug of scarcely suppressed laughter from Treasure. 'If you don't mind I'll sit here for a few minutes,' Scarbuck continued, moving towards a wooden bench. 'You two go ahead and I'll catch you up and walk a few holes with you later.'

After some mild but unconvincing protest from both Treasure and Speke-Jones, the two men moved back to the tee. His opponent invited Treasure to drive first.

The first hole at Mid-Stoke is a simple three hundred and twenty yard par four, with a 'dog-leg' to the left two-thirds of the way to the green. Treasure took the two wood from his bag, and with a perfectly co-ordinated swing drove the ball two hundred and fifty yards – a little more to the left than he had intended so that its final course took it perilously close to the edge of a bunker. It rolled up the lip of the trap without dropping in, trickled down the other side of the incline, stopping on flat ground some sixty yards short of the green.

Most of Treasure's golfing intimates would have uttered a good natured 'lucky' at this escape. Speke-Jones offered no such comment. 'Good shot,' he said, and sounded as though he meant it.

'Lucky finish, you mean.' Treasure smiled.

Speke-Jones shook his head. 'I'm not a great believer in luck, Mr Treasure, in golf or anything else for that matter. We're all captains of our own fate. I prefer making chances to taking them.' As if to illustrate the application of this philosophy he pointed to the number on the four wood he was holding.

Speke-Jones did not so much address the ball as consciously demonstrate the consecutive motions involved in a well-learned drill. His grip, stance and swing were copies of those frequently illustrated in the Sunday newspapers. He was insufficiently relaxed in play, yet he clearly did not extend himself to the full. His drive sent the ball an unimpressive hundred and fifty yards – but down the very centre of the fairway: a safe and sensible shot for a high handicap player with a stroke in hand against his opponent.

Treasure admired the control displayed by a golfer evidently high on application if low on natural aptitude. The banker was practised at reading character from the way a man played golf. What he had just witnessed fitted very well with his assessment of Speke-Jones. Cynically he wondered how high the stakes would need to be for the politician to take chances.

CHAPTER IX

The players halved the first hole. Treasure won the longer second. At the difficult third the politician had demonstrated his coolness under pressure and a continuing mature appreciation of his own limitations. Both players had reached the green in two. Treasure had just missed getting a 'birdie' three with a putt that obstinately halted at the very lip of the hole; Speke-Jones had also taken two putts.

'Well done; halved with no stroke for you,' said Treasure, smiling. 'Keep playing that kind of golf and they'll soon have your handicap down.'

'It's the stimulation and challenge of your example,' replied Speke-Jones seriously as they walked across to the fourth tee. 'I don't often play with people of your calibre, but they say that's the way to improve one's game.' He paused before adding with a touch more meaning, 'And that doesn't only apply to golf either.'

The fairway of the short fourth hole was littered with the persons of four very inexpert players, none of whom had reached the green with his drive nor even succeeded in following the most direct line of approach.

'We've caught up a bunch of rabbits,' Treasure observed testily. 'Perhaps they'll let us through at the next tee,' he added hopefully but without much conviction.

'Smoke?' Speke-Jones had seated himself on the bench provided against the eventuality they were facing.

Treasure refused a cigarette but noted the opulent Dupont lighter. 'Tell me about Forward Britain,' he said casually. 'Is it really your line of country?' There was a compliment suggested in his tone, implying that the two men shared an attitude that put both above involvement with sideshow pressure groups.

'Oh, you're right there,' agreed Speke-Jones with alacrity.

'It's a movement in search of a cause, you might say.'

'And a leader?'

Speke-Jones smiled. 'You could say that too. George Scarbuck isn't exactly heaven-sent in that connection, is he? Colourful, mind you . . . and there is good in the idea, of Forward Britain, I mean. This lurch to the left . . . there's bound to be a reaction sooner or later, and I can't see that coming in conventionally political form.'

Treasure weighed this piece of rationalization and found it made better sense as self-justification. Speke-Jones was a Labour Member of Parliament with dwindling credibility, who might himself soon be looking for a cause. A further 'lurch to the left' on the part of the Socialists might well leave him quite a long way to the right of centre, and certainly outside the party fold. Treasure found it difficult to accept that a cyclical reaction from the forces of the right would not express itself through conventional political channels; he could appreciate, however, that trimmers of Speke-Jones's type might find themselves washed out of main-stream politics if attitudes and parties polarized. He knew enough of Speke-Jones's political provenance to figure that the man would be unacceptable as a parliamentary candidate in any other party – and in any case he did not strike Treasure as the kind ready to persevere with the long haul back to credibility that inevitably faces the lesser breed of political turncoat.

'It's the rule of law, d'you see. Taken a hell of a knock over the last ten years.' Speke-Jones seemed almost to be talking to himself. 'If unemployment gets any higher they'll be pushing for increases in National Assistance, and where's the money to come from? Worker power is too strong now to be fobbed off with a reduction in the dole like the 'thirties.' He paused, and this time looked at Treasure. 'Mark my words, there'll be civil strife and the only thing standing between you and me and bloody revolution will be the loyalty of the police force and the army. Policemen and soldiers accept the rule of law because they live by it – and they're the only ones who do nowadays. But put them in a real crisis, and where's the leadership coming from to keep up morale and loyalty – not from my lot; workers are sacred cows to us whether they work or not. And as for the other bunch, God help us if the chips go down. I tell you, something has to be done . . . and I'm ready to do it,' he finished firmly.

Treasure not only caught the drift of this soliloquy; on consideration he thought he might actually be ahead of its implications. If Speke-Jones was openly allying himself with a new and evidently political movement, and at the same time freely denigrating the policy of the party he was elected to represent, he must already have estimated that the stakes were high enough to attract him into the game. But Treasure doubted that Speke-Jones would be ready to exchange the relative security of an 'also-ran' position in an established political party for anything less than the leadership of a hardly formed pressure group. Even accepting that the loss of his parliamentary seat would mark the end of Speke-Jones in conventional politics, the man had friends well placed in British industry, and Treasure did not doubt that these would provide him with a sufficient income through outside directorships and consultancy fees – indeed, he guessed some were doing so already.

If financial gain was not motivating Speke-Jones, then Treasure was experienced enough in such matters to conclude that power was the only possible alternative prize. And Speke-Jones had yet to enjoy real political power. He had never been afforded the meanest position under the Crown when his party was in office. Was this the cause of his disenchantment, his frustration, and his ambition? Was Speke-Jones casting himself in the Messianic role of the leader above ordinary politics, prepared to rescue Britain from the popularly threatened onset of nationwide anarchy if economic disaster did overtake the country?

Treasure even accepted that the scenario sketched by the politician was, in certain circumstances, a credible prediction. But he happened to have a very healthy regard for the rule of law himself, and no faith whatsoever in self-convinced dictators masquerading as saviours at the head of private armies.

'The green's clear; my honour, I think.' Speke-Jones was roughly jerked back into the present by Treasure's remark. This time the better player's near-perfect shot to the centre of the green was sadly unmatched by his opponent's ill-prepared, scuffed drive. Speke-Jones had lost his concentration – or more accurately he was preoccupied with something other than golf. Treasure won the hole easily, but the other's leap-frogging series of strokes to the green through thick rough had been time-consuming. They reached the next tee too late to be invited through by the players ahead who were once again spread out across the next fairway.

Treasure decided to employ the inevitable waiting time to some purpose. 'So you see the Forward Britain Movement as a vehicle for national survival? – bit puny, I'd have thought.'

'At the moment, yes – and it will take organizing, or reorganizing, but the basic structure's there already. You know there are three hundred thousand members?' Treasure did not know, and the number surprised him. 'And they're recruiting at the rate of a thousand a week – mostly disaffected middle-class people with a genuine grievance. They're the real losers, d'you see – galloping inflation, higher taxation, subsidies for the indolent, there's no end to it, except a reduction in living standards for people who've worked to improve their lot. The very rich are waterproof enough to ride out any storm.' Speke-Jones gave Treasure an almost apologetic glance. 'The so-called underprivileged have nothing to lose in the circumstances, and they think they've everything to gain. It's the people in the middle who are feeling the pinch – and they're about ready to fight back, offered some leadership. They'd vote for a real national government, given the chance, but they're not going to get it.'

'And you think Forward Britain would meet their aspirations?'

'Well, it's very broadly based for a start. All kinds of

people united by a common interest. This bunch Scarbuck's
get here today is pretty representative. There're a lot of
trade unionists involved – not the ones who live in council
houses, but the ones with mortgages, and that's the clue;
property ownership; something to defend.' Speke-Jones
hesitated before his next statement, then continued slowly,
as though weighing his words more carefully than before.
'You'd be surprised at the number of serving officers
involved . . . police too . . . people used to an ordered, disciplined life looking for leadership at national level and not
finding it. They're the ones who are most bitter about the
social drift – and fearful about its consequences.'

Treasure stooped to place a ball on the tee with this
Welsh rhetoric claiming more of his attention than he had
expected. He remained unconvinced about the role Speke-
Jones had in mind for Forward Britain, but he was disturbed
by some of the things he had been told. The suggestion that
commissioned officers in HM Forces might be knowingly
involved in a movement progressing to power outside the
democratic process he found absurd. He was more concerned
that such people might be unknowingly gathered into such
an organization at a point where its real aims were not
revealed.

Treasure had been aware of Forward Britain for some time
but had dismissed it as a fold for cranks, not a den of fanatics.
In his work he had enjoyed many civilized, intelligent
conversations with leaders of some of the resurgent countries.
It still disappointed if not surprised him that many such men
could be calm and sensible in private, then cruel and worse
than autocratic in their public utterances and actions. He
had an uneasy feeling that his rational companion might
belong to this breed, easily capable of explaining away the
need for stern dictatorial measures as the means for promoting
desirable, national ends. He wondered, too, if he had been
treated to the confidences he had just heard more in his
capacity as a banker than as a private citizen. He resolved
to find this out.

The fifth hole at Mid-Stoke, although only three hundred

yards long, involves a carry of a hundred and sixty yards over a valley of thick rough. Using his driver, Treasure sent the ball streaking low and long on to the fairway to finish not quite on the green but close to it.

'Magnificent,' said Speke-Jones, at the same time giving a sidelong glance at an alternative tee placed some thirty yards ahead and slightly to the left of the one they were using.

Although no tournament of any consequence had ever been played at Mid-Stoke, each hole was provided with three tees – Ladies, Players, and what the Club Committee presumed to call Championship. Out of habit, Treasure had selected the backward Championship tee at the first hole while waiting for Scarbuck and Speke-Jones. Now he realised that it would have been charitable to have given Speke-Jones the option at the beginning. To suggest that his opponent should play off a forward tee at this point in the game was an offer that Treasure was hardly ready to risk. Yet somehow he found himself making it.

Speke-Jones required no second bidding. 'Well, it is a long carry,' he said, trundling his bag and trolley to the other tee. Treasure concluded first that bankers lived sheltered lives, and secondly that Speke-Jones was the most unabashed opportunist he had met in a very long time – a view that was shortly to be reinforced.

Despite the advantage he enjoyed on the Player's tee, Speke-Jones failed to carry the rough. His ball lodged in a bank just below the fairway.

It was obvious to Treasure that his opponent had abandoned rather than lost the studied application he had demonstrated earlier in the game – undoubtedly because he had more important things on his mind. It was for this reason that Treasure felt no inhibition about putting a further question on what he would normally have felt an unfairly distracting subject. 'Who provides the funding for Forward Britain?' he enquired as the two walked down in the direction of Speke-Jones's ball. 'That is, if there's no secrecy involved,' he added.

Speke-Jones smiled. 'There's no secrecy, Mr Treasure. Members pay a minimum subscription of five pounds a year – and that's no widow's mite.'

Treasure mentally agreed. With three hundred thousand members, Forward Britain must already be enjoying an income, or capital build, of at least one and a half million pounds a year – substantial funding by any standards.

'And that's only the start,' Speke-Jones added. 'There's a further expectancy – what you might call an endowment – coming shortly. A sum in the region of three million.'

They had halted beside Speke-Jones's ball, but the player was not troubling to examine its position. He was gazing intently at Treasure's face looking for an outward manifestation of the reaction he knew his last remark must have provoked. But Treasure was too old a hand at money games to provide satisfaction.

Speke-Jones continued: 'That *is* in confidence Mr Treasure . . . but there's a good reason for my telling you. D'you see, we need an experienced banker . . . a highly respectable banker.' He paused. 'That's why I came here to meet you.'

CHAPTER X

'I wasn't meaning to destroy no evidence,' said Banquet sourly. 'Just doin' the job wot I was paid for – an' a proper job I done of it too.'

The evidence of his industry lay before them. Banquet, Chief Inspector Bantree, and Detective-Sergeant Wadkin were grouped around the neat and tidied mound that marked the resting place of Maggie Edwards. PC Humble stood behind them at what he judged a respectful distance – not from the grave, but from the figure of his superior.

Having been paid – in advance – the piece work rate of three pounds for the grave-filling job, Banquet had completed the task with zeal and speed. His apparent enthusiasm had been not unassociated with the fact that if he was through by three forty-five he knew he could be home in time to see the second half of the FA Cup Final on television. As it was, no sooner had he finished raking around the mound of the grave than he was descended upon by three policemen and ordered to desist.

'Not your fault, Mr Banquet, not your fault at all,' said Bantree reassuringly. 'If we'd realized what you were doing, and we should have done –' he gave his Sergeant a reproving glance – 'we'd have got to you sooner. Now you say the grave had been dug and prepared in the normal way?'

'So far as I could tell, yes,' Banquet replied, 'but I'm no expert. Gardenin's my job, not bloomin' gravediggin'. Boards weren't in place though. Reckon that's the larse thing 'Orace would'a done if 'ee'd finished the job 'iself.'

'Boards?' Bantree enquired.

'For restin' the coffin on afore it's lowered, like; they was 'ere orl right, but they wasn't laid out proper and ready.'

'And you think if Mr Worple had finished the work he'd have put the boards in position?'

'Sure 'ee would, an' the ropes as well. They was 'ere too – the ropes for lowerin' – but they wasn't made ready.'

'But the hole itself was finished – it was the right depth, levelled at the bottom and so on?'

'Clean as a whistle all through. Depth I don't know about, not bein' my job; 'ee looked deep enough – an' felt it with the in-fillin'.'

Sergeant Wadkin glanced at his notes. 'You said there were a lot of footmarks.'

Banquet sighed and looked at him sourly. 'Stan's to reason there'd be footmarks with twenty or more people payin' their respects at the funeral. I asked Vicar if 'ee wanted tarpaulin down afore the service, but 'ee said no 'cos the ground was dry. So it were left to me to rake up after – and rake up I done.'

It was Inspector Bantree's turn to sigh. The turfed and the bared ground around the grave were neat and clean. The possibility of finding footprints, other than possibly some of Banquet's, was very remote indeed. 'Thank you, Mr Banquet,' he said, 'I expect you'd like to be getting along. We'll be in touch if there's anything else.'

Banquet gathered up his things and made to go; then he turned back to the Inspector. 'If there's anythin' I can do to 'elp get 'im wot's done in 'Orace, you only 'as to say.' And with this final unexpected witness to amity he made his way across the churchyard.

Bantree smiled at the retreating figure before turning to his assistants. 'Now, Sergeant, this grave has to be undug, all the earth sieved – well, the routine's obvious. There should be enough coppers here in a minute to cope. We're still not sure where he died because we don't know for certain when he died – the time intervals are so short – but unless he was taken from here to Old Windsor by helicopter, and that's not likely, it's safe to assume he was done in right here, or certainly in this village. And it's murder we're investigating; whether he died of the stab wounds, or the broken back. Now come over here.' He motioned the Sergeant to the gate that led into Mitchell Hall. 'Constable Humble, you stay right there until the work party arrives. The policeman on the gate will keep out sightseers.'

Once out of Humble's hearing the Inspector, continued. 'I've cleared the exhumation with the Vicar and the dead person's daughter. No red tape; it's not a proper exhumation, we shan't be opening the coffin. See that it's put decently to one side, and if it can't go back tonight, store it in the ambulance that's coming. Now, a knife was brandished by a Filipino on the other side of this wall this morning – the Vicar told me that much, what's the rest of the story? Have you got the man?'

'No, sir; that is, I've seen him, and he's still available but he's accounted for from ten-thirty through to twelve-thirty.'

'Where was he?'

'In Reading General Hospital being X-rayed and treated for two broken ribs – courtesy of the Vicar.'

'Well, that's a new twist on the church militant.' Bantree

chuckled. 'And there are plenty of witnesses of course?'
The Sergeant nodded. 'What about the other Filipinos? I
gather there's a whole tribe of them – what are they here
for anyway?'

'Officially, sir, they're on holiday.' Bantree raised his
eyebrows. 'Actually they're digging a swimming pool for
Mr Scarbuck – part of a larger group brought over at
Mr Scarbuck's expense three weeks ago. The rest of the
party are staying near Scarborough, sir.'

'Enjoying their holiday?'

'Not really, sir, they're employed demolishing a country
house and laying out a new building estate.'

'Fiddle.'

'Precisely so, sir, but not one that need delay us now, I
thought . . . Detective-Constable Sheer will be making a
report, he's over there now, sir.'

Bantree nodded, as much in approval of Wadkin as of the
action he had taken. The Inspector liked Wadkin, who
was young, keen, and the product of one of the newer
universities noted more for its student militancy than as a
training ground for future officers of the law. Wadkin
seemed to have survived higher education and the statutory
period in the lower echelons of the Force without losing
the sense of initiative and public service that had presumably
attracted him to the job in the first place. He could have
moved in faster on Banquet; but then, so could have Bantree
himself.

'How many other Filipinos?'

'Eleven, sir; ten are accounted for during the relevant
time. They were working under the supervision of a Mr
Eustace Dankton.'

'Foreman?' (Poor Dankton!)

'In a way sir. Actually he's an antiquarian – the site is
an historical one and he's looking out for seventeenth-
century relics. But he was supervising the workers from
ten-thirty through to lunch time.'

'Reliable?'

'I should say so, sir.'

'Which leaves one Filipino unaccounted for.'

'Not entirely, sir. Two of them attacked the Vicar. One was sent to Reading injured, the other was just bruised and badly winded. He was ordered to lie down in the dormitory they have organized in the basement at the Hall. It seems he was still not fit for heavy work at three-thirty, but he was detailed to caddy for Mr Scarbuck at the Golf Club then.'

'Have you talked to him?'

'Not yet, sir; you see, we can't find him.'

Bantree looked at his watch. 'Have you tried the golf-course?'

'Sheer went over there, sir, and found Mr Scarbuck sitting on a seat near the Club House. It appears there was an altercation, sir. The caddy, he's known as Fred, apparently attacked Mr Scarbuck and ran away. He hasn't been seen since.'

'In what way did he attack Mr Scarbuck?'

'Violently, sir, according to the victim – butted him in the stomach with his head.'

'With or without provocation?'

'That's difficult to tell, sir. It appears Mr Scarbuck hit him with a golf-ball.'

'Hm, I suppose it depends on how fast it was moving.' Bantree paused. 'Anyway, there's one known belligerent Filipino at large and he's the closest thing we've got to a murder suspect. Find him. If he's still on foot he can't have got far.

'That's in hand, sir.'

'Right. I'm going over to the Hall. Join me when you've got the coffin out.' He looked toward the church's main gate. 'And here come the reinforcements, not before time.' A police van and two cars were drawing up alongside the churchyard wall. 'Is this gate open?'

'It is now, sir, but according to Mr Dankton it was locked by Mr Scarbuck at about ten-twenty – after the Vicar had climbed the wall. It was opened for a moment to let a dog through. Otherwise it's been locked all day until I came through from the Hall just now.'

'Dankton has a key?'

'Yes, sir, he let me through.'

'Right; see you later.' Bantree pushed open the gate.

The swimming pool site – the scene of furious activity earlier in the day – was now completely deserted. The neat excavation appeared to be complete, ready, Bantree assumed, for the concrete lining to be applied. He also surmised, correctly as it happened, that the next step would not be work for unskilled labourers supervised by an antiquarian. The whole of the west side was draped in tarpaulin, and a deep trench had been cut in the centre of the shallow north end running back some fifteen feet before it took a sharp turn to the left. Bantree knew enough about swimming pool plumbing to deduce that this ditch was destined to carry the pipe that would return filtered and probably heated water to the pool. He was prompted idly to consider how the water would be extracted for the purpose of filtration, then guessed that the tarpaulin hid the holes cut for this purpose.

'Chief Inspector Bantree?' Scarbuck had thrown open the centre venetian window on the ground floor of Mitchell Hall. The Inspector had been making for the front of the building, but he now changed direction towards the colourful figure – still dressed for golf – standing on the steps that led from the window to the terrace.

'I'm George Scarbuck; your sergeant said you'd be over. Come in, won't you?'

Bantree entered the long, high-ceilinged room which, like the famous double-cube room at Wilton, was the showpiece of Mitchell Hall. Scarbuck had purchased with the house most of the furniture and fittings imported by Moonlight three years earlier to provide the hoped-for tourists with something approaching the trappings and atmosphere of an historic salon. The effect was impressive, if a long way short of cosy.

'How's this for quality, Inspector?' said Scarbuck proudly.

'Very nice, sir, very nice indeed,' replied Bantree. He

smiled. 'Now how did you come to know my name, sir?'

'Your sergeant mentioned it, Inspector, and I make it my business never to forget a name that counts. As President of Forward Britain I happen to believe that senior policemen count for a great deal more than most in our community. Are you familiar with the Movement?'

'Broadly, sir, yes,' replied Bantree, whose steady promotion had been in some part assisted by his well-known penchant for political independence. 'I understand you have a rally on here this weekend.'

'Hardly a rally, Inspector, just a social get-together with some of the top chaps. We're having cocktails here in an hour's time followed by dinner. You'll be welcome to join us if you're free.'

'Very nice of you, Mr Scarbuck, but I'm afraid I'm likely to be on duty the rest of this evening. Sergeant Wadkin must have told you why we're here. I gather you've been helping him with our enquiries.'

'So far as I could, Inspector, but frankly I don't see how anyone from the Hall can be involved. Everyone's accounted for except one of the little Filipinos who are here helping out with the swimming pool – but he'll turn up. In any case, we all know where he was this morning.'

'So I understand, sir. Do you think I might have a word with Mr Dankton – I understand he was supervising the . . . er . . . helpers.'

'Of course, Inspector. I'll see if he's in his room.' Scarbuck moved to a house telephone incongruously positioned on a passable reproduction of an ornate Louis XV gaming table, the instrument somehow reducing what authenticity the piece possessed. 'I'm a great believer in good communications,' Scarbuck continued, 'had 'phones installed in all principal rooms the day we moved in. Ah, Eustace, I'm in the saloon with Chief Inspector Bantree; he'd like a word with you.' There was a pause for Dankton's reply. 'Well, never mind that, man, slip a dressing-gown on, we'll not stand on ceremony. Come now.' The last two words were issued as an order.

Scarbuck replaced the receiver. 'He was in the bath. By the by, Inspector, the party of Filipinos are going north by mini-coach this evening. You've no reason to refrain them, have you?'

'That's difficult to say at the moment, sir. I take it you are expecting all twelve to make the journey?'

'Ay, that's a point.' Scarbuck paused. 'But my guess is young Fred will be back within the hour, tail between his legs. He thinks I'm angry with him – I was too, little devil – but he'll show up.'

'Well, if he does sir, we shall want him for questioning.'

'I see. You know none of these chaps speak English, Inspector. Johnnie, the head boy, has a few words, but the others will be a dead loss for questioning – your sergeant found that out earlier.'

'Then I'm afraid we shall have to detain Fred until we can get hold of an interpreter. Ah, Mr Dankton, I presume?'

If appearances had been against Dankton in his open air role they did little to improve his image indoors. His tall, thin figure was now encased from neck to bare knees in a faded Paisley silk dressing-gown which, with the proper accessories, would have been suitable attire for a drawing-room entrance in a 1930's comedy. Held together, as it was now, with a belt borrowed from a fawn raincoat, it lacked both the style and the sophistication required for its wearer easily to carry off a relaxed arrival. But the garment, and his bare feet, were witness that Dankton had come without delay. Bantree had no way of telling whether the man's deathly pallor was normal.

'Any sign of Fred yet?' asked Scarbuck brusquely. Dankton shook his head in reply. His hands too were shaking, though Bantree was unable to decide whether this was the result of apprehension or a too prompt arrival from a warm bath into a comparatively cold drawing-room.

'I'm sorry to inconvenience you, Mr Dankton,' said the Inspector, 'but there are a few more questions we'd like you to answer about this morning. Besides the Filipinos you were supervising, did you see anyone else – anyone –

around the swimming pool or the churchyard this morning between ten-thirty and noon?'

Dankton hesitated before replying – long enough to ponder the question or long enough to invent a lie; once again Bantree was not sure.

'No, no one,' said Dankton finally, staring at the carpet and clasping his hands more tightly before him. 'I was there the whole time; there was no one.'

There was a tap on the window through which Bantree had been admitted. Sergeant Wadkin beckoned to the Inspector from outside.

'Excuse me a moment, will you?' said Bantree. He joined Wadkin outside, closing the glass door behind him.

'Pathologist's report, sir – makes a difference to our enquiries. Thought I'd better bring it over right away. Worple died between ten-thirty and ten-forty-five. Cause of death spinal fractures consistent with a fall from a height of ten to twenty feet on to a hard and uneven surface.'

'How deep was that grave?' Bantree's gaze moved across to the swimming pool excavation. 'No, we can forget that; it couldn't have been more than eight feet, and that chap Banquet would have told us if the bottom was filled with rocks. The pool's deep enough, though.'

'I just looked at the deep end, sir. The floor's earthy but there's a good deal of broken stone piled at the side.'

'What do they say about the stab wounds?'

'Not stab wounds, sir, lacerations from pairs of revolving and probably half-circular blades, possibly attached to a mechanical instrument. The wounds were inflicted immediately after death, eight in all in the chest and abdomen.'

Bantree was used to unlikely deductions from forensic boffins. 'They mean he was run over by a lawn-spiker?'

'Not so far off the mark, sir. They seem to think it could have been an implement of that sort but bigger, and probably not power-operated. The stab cuts are in two even rows across the body, but the pairs of lacerations are of uneven depth.' Wadkin was reading from a typed report in his hand.

The Inspector remained unimpressed. 'Yes, well I saw

the wounds. Certainly they were ragged, and they were
in pairs, but they could have been made by a man with a
broad knife, or spike, and a rhythmic swing, running out of
energy or sadistic inclination. Sergeant, I want you to find
that missing Filipino – and fast.'

Wadkin made off into the twilight. Before re-entering
Mitchell Hall, Bantree paused to wonder why anyone killed
by a fall should then be mutilated, transported twenty miles,
deposited inside a cabin cruiser, and set alight. 'Camouflage,'
he said to himself. 'The real question is did he fall or was he
pushed?' Which, despite the Inspector's experience and
acuity, wasn't the question at all.

CHAPTER XI

Treasure hurried into the Dower House at ten minutes
to six. Speke-Jones had lost the match at the seventh hole,
and the banker had no difficulty in persuading him to aban-
don the game at that point.

Scarbuck had not reappeared on the golf-course so that
there had been no opportunity to raise the subject of his
parting with Mitchell Hall. Concern on this account served
to deepen Treasure's unease as he now reconsidered events
he had tried to put out of his mind until he had the opportunity to confront his host. He had cut short any discussion
on the subject of his becoming banker for the Forward
Britain Movement by explaining it was a rule at Grenwood,
Phipps that no director of the bank would serve any political
organization as an honorary officer in a financial capacity – a
factually true statement. He had gone on to suggest that if
the Movement was in need of the advice normally provided
by merchant bankers, then a formal approach should be
made by an authorized agent of the group to his board in
the City – and not, he had implied, to one director of that
board, by an unaccredited politician on a golf-course.

In ordinary circumstances Treasure would have been

perfectly happy broadly to entertain the proposition Speke-
Jones had made to him – notwithstanding the house-rule he
had quoted. Simply, in this instance, he had erected a corporate barricade behind which to take refuge. He was fairly
certain that this was one piece of business Grenwood,
Phipps could do without, but he was concerned not to be
precipitate in the matter. Deep down, he also admitted to
himself a certain curiosity about the financial affairs of
Forward Britain, which a formal approach would almost
certainly assuage without commitment.

Treasure had not pressed Speke-Jones to support the
surprising statement that the politician's presence at Mitchell
Stoke was accounted for entirely by his own decision to spend
the weekend with the Moonlights. Twenty-four hours before
he had not been aware himself that he would be visiting
Oxfordshire the next day. He took this episode as yet further
evidence of Speke-Jones's penchant for instant opportun-
ism.

'Is that you, Mark darling?' Elizabeth Moonlight appeared
on the first-floor gallery that spanned the width of the hall
where Treasure was standing. 'Heavens, I must look a mess.'
One hand patted some slightly dishevelled hair, then went to
smooth the folds of the long white lace negligee that elegantly
enveloped the small slim figure.

'I've done what I can for Worple's daughter,' Elizabeth
continued, 'but one feels so inadequate confronted by real
tragedy. Then I was interrogated, my dear, by a rather
attractive young police sergeant. Anyway, he seemed satisfied
that *I* didn't murder poor Mr Worple – and that Arthur
couldn't have either. I suppose they have to begin by sus-
pecting everybody. Now I must get dressed for dinner.'
She continued in a stage whisper, 'Aggie insists on helping
which means everything will take longer.'

Aggie was the sole surviving Moonlight family retainer.
Now well into her seventies, she had long since been officially
retired, but having no home of her own had been invited to
stay on in the household. Almost deaf and extremely decrepit,
her well-intentioned desire to be of assistance at dinner

parties resulted always in her being of more hindrance than
help. Even so, it was not in Elizabeth Moonlight's nature to
deny her the satisfaction of making some return for the
kindness she received.

'Oh, one other thing, Mark.' Elizabeth returned to the
balustrade as Treasure went to mount the stairs. 'There
was a 'phone call for you about an hour ago – nice man called
Jumbo Cranton with a deep brown voice; said we'd met at
Henley years ago. I think I remember him . . . isn't he a
builder?'

Treasure laughed aloud. 'Well, you could call him that,
and you did meet him five years ago when his son was in the
Shrewsbury Eight – though I recall his paying more attention
to you than he did to the rowing.'

'Flatterer! Anyway, will you ring him? I put the number
on the pad by the 'phone in the study – Arthur's not back
yet. Now I *must* fly.' She disappeared in a flurry of lace.

Sir James Crib-Cranton was chairman of the biggest
civil engineering and construction group in the country –
and, for that matter, in practically any other country as well.
He was one of Treasure's closest friends, though this was not
the reason why Treasure went to telephone him on the
instant. Crib-Cranton's company was one of Grenwood,
Phipps & Co.'s largest clients and Treasure doubted he was
being sought out on a Saturday in the country for a friendly
chat.

'My dear Mark, a thousand apologies for breaking into
your tête-à-tête with the delectable Lady Moonlight. Molly's
still away, I assume!' The good humoured innuendo in the
opening was no less than Treasure had expected. Crib-
Cranton had been divorced three times and had convinced
himself, if no one else, that this was singular proof he was
no secret philanderer – a role he ascribed to all those males
of his acquaintance who, in his terms, gave the appearance of
remaining faithful to one wife.

'I'm enjoying a bachelor weekend with Arthur and
Elizabeth, if that's what you mean,' replied Treasure
woodenly. 'By the way, Elizabeth had some difficulty

remembering who you were.' The deflating of his friend's ego was the surest way of stemming his banter.

'Well, none of them is perfect,' said Crib-Cranton, undefeated, and then, changing the subject, 'You know, it's the most extraordinary coincidence your being where you are. I rang you at home this morning after reading in *The Times* that the Kuwaiti talks have been cancelled – needed your advice and thought you'd still be about. Your house-keeper said you were at Mitchell Stoke. Extraordinary coincidence.'

'Why, Jumbo? – weekend advice is expensive.' Treasure was used to humouring captains of British industry but he knew this one well enough to bring him to the point without too much ceremony.

Crib-Cranton took the hint. 'We were approached yester-day to rescue an outfit called Scarbuck Construction – land-bank, plant, existing contracts, mile high tax losses, the lot, going for a song if we act before the banks put the bailiffs in on Tuesday. It looks interesting from our view-point, and for reasons I won't waste time on now. We've had full disclosure of the relevant bumf – my people worked all night on it. Usual cash flow problem, nothing out of the ordinary for a middle-sized concern these days, and potentially very profitable if they can hang on for a year or so. The two directors who came to see me last evening seemed competent, but there's a problem.'

Treasure had a suspicion he had met that same problem earlier in the day. 'Go on, Jumbo,' he said.

'They – the other directors, that is – are in open rebellion against the chairman; want to ditch him.'

'Because he spends too much time organizing the Forward Britain Movement?'

'Ah, you know about him. Well, partly that, but more important the fellow's a crook.' Treasure gave an inward sigh at the familiarly incautious way in which Jumbo Cranton transmitted highly slanderous comments on open telephone lines.

'Jumbo, you shouldn't say such a thing.' An automatic

comment from a prudent financier.

'Well, I've said it, and don't be so bloody prissy because I've got proof of misappropriation of funds right here in my hand.'

'Misappropriation for personal use?'

'Good as. In the last nine months he's siphoned off nearly half a million quid in unsecured loans to Forward Britain Enterprises, Ltd – a private company which he personally owns outright.'

'But he couldn't have done that without at least his chief accountant knowing, and what about the auditors?'

'Fiddlesticks! You know what some of these autocratic company chairmen get away with short term. And that's the trick. The whole thing's been rigged inside one financial year. The loans were to be repaid this week in time for the annual audit which begins next week – purposely delayed by Scarbuck, I might add. The financial director's beside himself because he thinks he could be implicated . . . complicity and all that. He and the other directors knew about the loans, but they're all Scarbuck's creatures – or they have been up to now – and they hold only about two per cent of the equity between them . . . frightened they might lose their jobs if they hollered. Now, of course, some of them at least are more frightened at the prospect of going to jug. Incidentally, Scarbuck has a majority holding in the show.'

'How much does the company owe the banks?'

'Oh, about fifteen million, but that's a separate matter. Most of the money is well enough secured against land, work in progress, and so on, and there are perfectly legitimate reasons for their applying for another three or four million – the banks won't play though, and worse still they're calling in some of the money they've already advanced. It's the usual story – Bank of England's got the jitters about the pound and the Big Four are reacting by clobbering corporate customers. We can pick the thing up all right . . . might mean a rights issue for us, but the institutions will play when they see the quality of the merchandise – Scarbuck's have some very impressive contracts, and no fixed price stuff either. But we don't want to pick up a scandal in the process.'

'And the other directors don't believe Scarbuck himself will repay the half million in time for the audit?'

'Well, he's running it bloody close, old boy. No, they obviously don't think he can pay up or they wouldn't be panicking, would they?'

'You know Scarbuck lives here?'

'That's why I rang . . . extraordinary coincidence your being where you are. Have you met the chap?'

'Yes, this afternoon. Listen, Jumbo, if your people like the look of Scarbuck Construction, keep them studying the paperwork over the weekend. I'll be in the office on Monday and if you're still of a mind to take on the company, from what you've told me I would guess we can hold off the banks for a week or two. If Scarbuck controls the company, obviously he has to consent to its being taken over, but if the banks are threatening to put in receivers I don't see he has any option, unless there's another bidder. The loan to Forward Britain is a quite separate matter. I'm guessing, but Scarbuck may be in a position to repay sooner than his colleagues think – but I'm only guessing.'

'You know something?'

'Not for certain. Is there a Speke-Jones on the board of either Scarbuck Construction or Forward Britain Enterprises?'

'Hang on, I'll look.' Treasure could hear Crib-Cranton shuffling papers at the other end of the line. 'You mean the MP chap? Nasty bit of work.' Treasure sighed audibly. 'No, he's not on the board of Scarbuck's and there are only two directors of the other outfit, Scarbuck himself and Anne Emily Scarbuck, probably his wife.'

'Right, I'll call you first thing Monday morning.'

'Thanks awfully, Mark. I really am sorry to have burst into your weekend. Don't neglect the lady now!' Crib-Cranton replaced the receiver before Treasure could parry this parting shot. He put down the telephone, then stared at it for a moment while he wove the story he had just heard into the web of information and conjecture in his mind already.

If Speke-Jones had been telling the truth, then the Forward Britain Movement had funds considerably in excess of half a million pounds. If this was the case, then Forward Britain Enterprises, Ltd – obviously some kind of management company the wily Scarbuck had set up to provide services to the Movement – would have little difficulty in finding funds to repay Scarbuck Construction. But if this was so, why had the money been borrowed in the first place? Could it be that Scarbuck had already gone through the Movement's funds, which Speke-Jones had suggested might exceed one and a half million? Or were the officers of the Movement – amongst whom Speke-Jones was presumably included – less co-operative about shifting money into Forward Britain Enterprises, Ltd than were the directors of Scarbuck Construction, Ltd – until recently an evidently obedient group of Scarbuck pawns? And what about the three million pound 'expectancy' referred to by Speke-Jones? Scarbuck himself had exhibited none of the forebodings and depression that would normally assail a man whose company was in imminent danger of foreclosure – nor the typical apprehension of someone facing a possible criminal charge in the fairly near future.

'Mark, Elizabeth said you were anxious to see me. What's all this about Worple being murdered?' Arthur Moonlight was standing in the doorway to the study. He looked grave and worn – graver and far more worn than the instant intelligence of Worple's fate could possibly have made him.

The American took the telephone from its cradle the moment it began to ring. 'Yes?'

'Les, what went wrong? They've found the body; the place is alive with police.'

'We got landed with a dead body, that's what went wrong. But it must have been in ashes – how did they trace it back here so fast?'

'It wasn't ashes, Les, and why did you start a fire anyway –

it wasn't necessary. We agreed . . .'

'Because the gasoline was there, and it seemed like a good idea at the time. Burned-up corpses are harder to trace than whole ones.'

'Les, everybody's being questioned . . .'

'So what? They've got nothing on you. You saw nothing; you know nothing. So don't panic; they're a day ahead of us, that's all, and by this time tomorrow I'll be half way to the States. There's enough to keep them guessing till then. Are the Flips out of the way?'

'I don't think so . . . there's one missing. The police think he did in the gravedigger.'

'Great, that'll keep the cops occupied. Let's hope he stays missing. Are the others allowed to leave?'

'I'm not sure . . . Les, the police are getting an interpreter.'

'Who speaks Sulu? – they've got to be kidding. There can't be anyone in the Embassy with ten words. Say, I guess they're opening the grave?'

'Yes.'

'Well, that follows, but if you did it right they're not gonna figure it. What time are you going in?'

'Around midnight – that's if the police have gone.'

'They'll have gone – what can they find after dark? Anyway it's raining. Just go carefully. Are you sure you don't want me there?'

'Quite sure. I can manage – the last bit's easy, and I've got all night. I'm telling everybody the good news before lunch tomorrow. I'll put your stuff in the car tonight.'

'OK – but our side gets half the price of the manuscript as well. I've seen Scarbuck. He'll split fifty-fifty or everybody's going to know where the thing was really found. Has he said anything to you about it?'

'You've seen him? No, he hasn't said anything. Les, when did you see him?'

'This afternoon; but don't worry, baby. I know we agreed I shouldn't meet him, but what's the difference at this stage? So I'll expect you here at the cottage around seven-thirty in the morning as arranged. If the cops are back, you're going to the eight a.m. mass at Pangbourne.'

'Yes . . . Les, I'm worried that Scarbuck . . .'

'Well, stop worrying; just get the stuff out, and make sure that raft comes down when you exit. Bye.'

CHAPTER XII

Timothy Trapp and Thelma Goodbody knelt together in the cellar of the vicarage gazing fixedly at one corner of the large canvas. Bach sat reverently – and more comfortably than the others – at his master's side waiting for something to happen that would mark the end of these devotions. Since nothing did – and since it was a time in the day when no one ever invited him to take exercise – he slowly let his eyes close and quietly went to sleep – no mean accomplishment while remaining in an upright position.

The painting still lay face upwards in the centre of the cellar floor. Familiarity had done nothing to improve Trapp's opinion of the piece as a work of art. In fairness, rubbing away one part of the picture was hardly the way to enhance the appearance of what remained, but the perplexed expressions on the faces of the two were not caused by any sense of vandal guilt.

During the course of the day Trapp had twice worked white spirit into the same small section of the canvas. Wiping away the first dose had revealed a whitened surface beneath the brown paint removed on the cloth. The second application, administered just twenty minutes before, had dissolved what appeared to be a solid white undercoat but failed to uncover the bare canvas Trapp had expected would lie beneath. On the contrary, paint of various hues now stood revealed, under a thick, resistant varnish, on the twenty-or-so square inches of the treated canvas, and at the top of the patch some clear, black script spelled *'eques fecit'*.

'Does it mean a horse did it?' enquired Trapp, who had no illusions about his lack of classical scholarship.

'No, not a horse,' said his companion, 'but it could mean a mounted person . . . or a knight. I'm not absolutely sure, Timothy, and I ought to be . . . sorry. I'll bet there's a proper signature above that inscription.'

'Well, let's clean off a bit more of the top coats then,' suggested Trapp heartily.

'Timothy – ' Miss Goodbody was suppressing the excitement she felt but she spoke loud enough to prompt Bach into opening one eye – 'I want you to promise me you won't put any more of that spirit on this picture. People didn't put Latin inscriptions on paintings much after the seventeenth century, and painters who were knighted were mostly good at it – very good.'

'You mean you think we could be on to something hot?'

'Jolly well boiling, if you want my guess – and it's not entirely a guess either.' Miss Goodbody had spent the previous several weeks reading up the history of Mitchell Hall and the Moonlight family to some purpose. She was now experiencing alternate pangs of horror and elation that the Vicar of Mitchell Stoke might have been employed that day in attempting literally to liquidate the work of Sir Anthony Vandyck. She briefly explained to Trapp the story of the Sarah Moonlight portrait and its disappearance in 1645.

Trapp viewed the canvas with a new respect. 'If it is a Vandyck it'll fetch enough to rebuild the Youth Club in . . .'

'Several youth clubs, wherever you want them,' interrupted Miss Goodbody firmly, 'but in the first place we don't *know* it's a Vandyck and in the second place, even if it is, it won't be yours.'

'I don't see that that follows,' said Trapp loftily. 'I found the thing; it's part of the vicarage . . . so to speak. Must have been here for years. Dammit, mice could have eaten it before now and who'd have been the wiser?' He finished with less assurance in his voice than had been evident at the start. This was the kind of argument he had used on parochial church councils, archdeacons, and once on an ecclesiastical court, on different occasions since he had become a priest, always to justify the exchange of passive impedimenta for active good works. 'There'll be problems, of course,' he added lamely.

'And the first one involves getting the picture cleaned properly,' said Miss Goodbody, briskly rising to her feet. 'Have you got an Oxford telephone directory upstairs?' Trapp nodded. 'Then I'm going to ring a friend of mine who works at the Ashmolean. He might be willing to come out here tonight or tomorrow – and anyway he can tell us what to do about the bit you've cleaned already . . . we don't want that dissolving overnight.' She was already half way up the stairs, with Bach close behind, hoping to be involved in the preparation of dinner.

'Thelma?'

'Yes, Timothy?'

'Could you sort of get your friend to keep the thing secret and . . . er . . . could you not tell anyone else here about it yet?'

'Yes, Timothy.' She hesitated on the top step, leaning back over the banister to give Trapp a reassuring, conspiratorial grin. The retriever, prevented from making further progress on the narrow stairway, settled on the step below, and adopted a bored expression. The girl went on, 'And I'll help you work out a more convincing story than the Bristol one too – but this isn't quite the same, you know. If that really is Sarah's picture, then it's not church property; it belongs to the Moonlights.'

Trapp reflected on this remark and decided he would rather argue the merits of rebuilding a burnt-out youth club with Arthur Moonlight than with any diocesan board of finance he had yet had the misfortune to encounter.

The human object of Trapp's charitable thoughts lowered himself into a wing chair in the Dower House study. 'So it's murder all right – and a harmless chap like that.'

'Yes, Arthur, but, as I said, the police are satisfied no one from here could have been involved – nor from the Hall either so far as I know.'

Moonlight lifted his eyes. 'I wonder, Mark. I wonder.'

'Oh come, I know you don't much care for Scarbuck, but I doubt he's a murderer,' said Treasure lightly. 'Anyway, he was probably right here in this room at the time of the crime.'

'Yes, and he left pretty sharply too.'

Treasure hesitated. 'D'you have any reason to suppose that Scarbuck was involved? Because if you do we ought to tell the police.' Moonlight shook his head. 'And there's nothing going on here – that you know of – that could harm you or Elizabeth if it came out?'

'What an extraordinary question – and the answer is certainly not.'

'Good,' replied Treasure. 'Then there's something I have to tell the police right away. I was threatened early this afternoon outside the Hall gates by a blond young man who drove away in a yellow VW.'

'Threatened? In what way threatened?'

Treasure related the details of his brief encounter. 'I think the chap must have mistaken me for Scarbuck – though I can't imagine why.'

'Were you dressed as you are now?'

'Yes, I changed for lunch if you remember . . .' Treasure's voice trailed off as his hand went to the white tie he was wearing to complement the dark blue shirt and blazer – the blazer he had worn for the meal and exchanged for a red sweater before his walk afterwards. Speke-Jones, on first acquaintance, had appeared to assume that Treasure might be, as he had put it, 'one of us'. The banker now realized he might inadvertently have given rise to this assumption through his appearance – red sweater, white tie, blue shirt. If Speke-Jones had jumped to the conclusion that Treasure had adopted the colours and the cause, then the belligerent stranger might well have made the worse error of taking Treasure for the leader of Forward Britain.

'So that's it all right,' said Moonlight. 'You enjoyed the dubious privilege of being mistaken for Scarbuck. But what did the chap mean about an accident, d'you suppose?

If there had been an accident here this morning we'd have known about it.'

'We do know there was a murder, though. Arthur, the boat-house in Old Windsor to which the body was taken . . . it belonged to Canwath-Wright.'

'Freddy? Good God!'

'You know him pretty well?' Treasure measured his words carefully.

'Of course I do, and so does everybody else who's worth a damn in archaeology . . . What are you getting at? Mark, are you suggesting this involves me with Worple's death, because if you are you can think again. Anyway, there's somebody much more closely associated with Freddy . . .' Moonlight stopped in mid-sentence, then, after a pause, he continued. 'Mark, I think you should tell the police about the chap who accosted you, and you can certainly tell them about my knowing Freddy Canwath-Wright – tell 'em myself, come to that. As it happens, I haven't seen or talked to Freddy for more than a year.'

'And you don't know anyone associated with Scarbuck in business or . . .'

'No, I do not, and why the hell should I? As far as I'm concerned Scarbuck's the outsider who bought the Hall. I know nothing about him or his friends, and the sooner I can get him out of the Hall the better.'

Treasure found most of what Moonlight had said more than necessarily defensive, but in general he was relieved at what he had heard. Much as he would have liked to press his friend on who it was that owned a closer association with Canwath-Wright, he had more important questions to put, and Moonlight's last remark reminded him of the promise he had made earlier in the day.

'I'm sorry, I did my best to corner Scarbuck this afternoon, but things didn't work out. We arranged to play golf, but he became a casualty early in the game.'

'Nothing trivial, I hope,' Moonlight muttered sourly. 'Surprised the chap knows one end of a golf-club from the other.'

'As a matter of fact he doesn't . . . Tell me, when he paid you for the Hall in the first place, was the cheque drawn on Scarbuck Construction?'

'No, it wasn't. I noticed it because that was one cheque I couldn't afford to have bounce . . . more's the pity it didn't, though.' Moonlight paused. 'It was drawn on Forward Britain Incorporated or Consolidated . . .'

'Forward Britain Enterprises?' Treasure interrupted eagerly.

'That's it . . . Thought it was odd at the time, but didn't question the chap – like looking a gift horse in the mouth. At least it was the way I felt then.'

'And what's really happened to alter your view, Arthur? Dammit, the man couldn't have been any more attractive then than he is now, though I admit he doesn't improve on acquaintance.' Treasure watched his host as he phrased the next question. 'Is it anything to do with the death of that old lady in the churchyard?'

It was easy to see that Moonlight's emotional reaction to this went deeper than mild surprise. 'Mark, you're a very observant chap – you're also a very old friend so you'll oblige me by accepting I can't answer that question.'

There was a stony silence in the room as both men considered the ambiguity in Moonlight's reply. Treasure eventually gave a sigh of resignation and glanced at his watch. 'Well, if I'm going to bare my soul to the police before dinner I'd better get moving. One other thing, Arthur: did Scarbuck know I was going to be here today?'

Moonlight rose, gathering up some books and a small parcel he had deposited earlier on a side table. 'Yes, he did. When you said you were coming I rang him last evening and invited him over for coffee this morning . . . mentioned you might be here; idea was to have you assess the chap before you set about doing my dirty work for me.' He gave Treasure an acutely embarrassed glance. 'It wasn't true what I said earlier about my intending to make him an offer myself – I was sure you'd be better at handling him. It didn't work, though; he left just before you arrived.'

Treasure nodded. So Speke-Jones could have been telling the truth about the reason for his own presence at Mitchell Stoke.

The two men moved towards the door of the study. Treasure put a hand on Moonlight's shoulder. 'Cheer up, Arthur. It's possible – just possible – Scarbuck will have to sell you back the Hall. I can't tell you more at the moment, in fact it's a breach of confidence to tell you anything at all, but friend Scarbuck may be in a pack of trouble. What you've told me about the cheque could be important.'

'You mean there's something phoney about this Forward Britain outfit?'

'Something like that.'

'And I really am sorry the thing slipped my mind when we talked earlier, Inspector.'

'Oh, better late than never, Mr Treasure. Perhaps a talk with Sir Arthur on his return helped to jog your memory.' Inspector Bantree delivered this piercing verbal shaft with disarming equanimity. The two men were standing beside Bantree's Ford which was parked behind an official police car outside the gates of Mitchell Hall.

'You'd recognize the man again, sir?'

'Without question.'

'And you say he's not known to Sir Arthur whom you very sensibly consulted on the matter before coming to see me?' Treasure nodded to the question and fought against the withering sense of guilt produced by the Inspector's words, despite the wan smile that accompanied them. 'And I expect you asked Sir Arthur whether he knew of anyone called Stacey, sir?'

'I did, as a matter of fact – and he doesn't.' Treasure attempted to imply that his precautionary talk with Moonlight had been conducted in a spirit of earnest helpfulness. He had not mentioned his host's friendship with Canwath-Wright.

'Well, that saves me troubling Sir Arthur – ' Treasure sighed inwardly – 'at the moment, sir. Now we'll have to find out whether anyone else in the village got a sight of your blond chap.'

For a moment Treasure had the distinct impression that the Inspector had reservations about the veracity of the whole story – and a quite irrational feeling that the policeman suspected it had been invented, and not simply delayed, in order to protect Moonlight.

'Yellow Volkswagens are pretty common, sir. You didn't by any chance notice the licence number?'

'No, Inspector.'

'No, sir.' Bantree nodded understandingly.

'But Miss Goodbody may have noticed it . . . She saw the car, and so did the people driving the funeral cars this afternoon.' Treasure plunged further into the detailed corroboration that had suddenly occurred to him. 'And Miss Goodbody thought the same car passed us, heading for the M4, on the far side of Pangbourne this morning.'

'At about what time, sir?'

'Oh, around eleven – perhaps a bit before.'

'She didn't notice a body in the back, sir?' The tone was matter-of-fact; not breathlessly expectant.

'No, but I see what you mean, Inspector – the time fits, doesn't it?'

'Pretty precisely, sir,' replied Bantree in the manner Treasure felt he would use for humouring infants. 'Now is there anything else you feel you'd like to tell me at this point, sir?'

Treasure swallowed. 'Look, Inspector . . . no, no there's nothing more. I really am sorry about being so dilatory. But the man said quite distinctly he'd be staying around.'

'I noted that, sir. Most helpful. Well then, I needn't delay you further.' Following a friendly nod to soften an almost curt dismissal, Bantree moved towards the police car which was occupied by a single uniformed constable.

Treasure walked back to the Dower House with a considerably lighter step, and not simply because he wanted to get out of the rain which had just begun to fall in defiance of the forecast. His concern that Moonlight might somehow be connected with the murder had evaporated – nor did he have any misgivings about what he had omitted to tell Bantree. During the conversation it had suddenly occurred to him who else it was – being worth more than a damn in archaeology – who could very likely claim acquaintance with Canwath-Wright. But for the first time he was given to wondering why Moonlight appeared almost studiously to ignore the presence of Eustace Dankton at Mitchell Stoke. By all accounts, the two men had a great deal in common, and it would have been natural for Moonlight to befriend – even to court – such a reasonably celebrated fellow scholar.

The fact that Dankton was in the employ of Scarbuck might have coloured Moonlight's attitude to some degree, but the man was so evidently out of sympathy with his employer that this fact alone hardly explained why Moonlight appeared not to acknowledge his presence.

CHAPTER XIII

'Now, Bishop, you know Mark Treasure already, and this is Miss Goodbody who's a friend of Timothy's.' Elizabeth Moonlight in a simple black angora dinner gown was escorting Bishop Wringle and his wife around the company assembled and sipping sherry in the comfortable drawing-room of the Dower House.

'How d'you do, my dear,' said the diminutive ecclesiastic in a high-pitched voice that both betrayed and nicely complemented his eighty years. He grasped Miss Goodbody's hand in both of his, showing no inclination to release it again. 'Staying at the vicarage, are you?' He beamed approvingly at Trapp across the room.

'No, Bishop,' replied Thelma Goodbody, promptly to confirm – in particular to a bishop – that Trapp's moral rectitude was above suspicion in at least one context. 'I'm at The Jolly Boatman.'

'What a waste,' said Clarence Wringle, though it was not clear to the others whether this was a reproof to Trapp or a comment on the girl's anatomy. Miss Goodbody looked crisp and becoming in a pink blouse, a wide black belt, and a long, dark green skirt.

'And this is Mrs Wringle,' went on the hostess firmly. The Bishop still held Miss Goodbody's hand.

'Call me Clara, please,' protested the tall, stout lady in a solid baritone. 'My turn to shake hands, Clarence,' she boomed in her husband's ear. The Bishop released his grip, gave his wife a pained look, and adjusted his hearing aid.

Although retired some ten years before, and after nearly half a century in the mission fields of Africa, neither the Bishop nor his wife looked spent. They were as oddly matched in appearance as they had been well suited in life. The tiny, bald prelate wore gaiters – a habit he affected on formal occasions in England even though he had never owned such distinguishing garments in all the time he had worked abroad; he found them warmer than trousers. His wife personified what a pillar of the church should be, morally by example, and physically by chance – though some thought by divine intent. She was draped in a floral silk gown of generous cut and uncertain vintage which added to its owner's already regal air; this in turn served to give her gaitered consort the appearance of a superannuated page.

The Wringles had settled at Mitchell Stoke sentimentally because the Bishop had been born at the vicarage, and gratefully because the cottage they occupied had been leased to them on very generous terms by Arthur Moonlight.

'Thelma is busy proving that Shakespeare put on *As You Like It* in our garden,' said Elizabeth, who was determined that the subject of murder should not be the main topic of the evening.

'We were wondering if you'd ever come across anything that might throw light on the subject, Bishop,' volunteered Trapp.

'I'm not as old as all that,' replied Wringle with a high-pitched cackle, 'but there are pointers, yes, there are pointers.

Anything come out of those diaries, Arthur?'

'What diaries?' questioned Trapp and Miss Goodbody simultaneously.

The Bishop put a hand to his mouth in mock dismay. 'My dear Arthur, have I disclosed a secret?'

'Not a secret exactly,' Moonlight replied, and then, addressing the company in general, 'Before we broke up the library when we moved here, I put aside some bound manuscripts that later turned out to be the diaries of Sarah Moonlight. Some years are missing but they cover roughly the period just before the Commonwealth, her time in exile – or some of it – and then from 1660 to the middle of '65.'

'Unique documents,' observed Mrs Wringle solemnly.

'Unique in the sense they're original and unpublished, but there were a great many more observant diarists of the period. Someone in the family obviously considered they were worth preserving – the bindings are early nineteenth-century. Unfortunately, whoever it was forgot to have them titled, and in consequence they'd been sitting unnoticed in the library all through my lifetime, and I'd guess my father's too.'

'Arthur was good enough to let me peek at some of them,' the Bishop interrupted. 'Fascinating, fascinating . . . She was . . . er . . . quite a girl, as they say.'

'She was no saint,' said Moonlight bluntly, 'and certainly unworthy of an apparently faithful and devoted husband.'

'One of Charles the Second's mistresses while he was abroad,' said the Bishop with authority and evident glee. 'Pepys said he had seventeen, though I've never been able to understand how he was able to be so specific about the number.' He stared at the bottom of his empty sherry glass as though he expected illumination from that source.

'And Charles was not the only one in receipt of her favours,' continued Moonlight almost savagely, indicating that he, at least, was concerned for the honour of his Royalist ancestor. 'That's why the diaries are of so little historical use; they read more like a whore's log-book.'

'How super,' said Miss Goodbody – and then wished she hadn't.

'But there must be some contemporary references of interest to us today.' This was Treasure.

'Yes, and I had the idea we might edit the thing down to one volume for publishing – but it'll be damn slim when the smut's cut out.'

'That reminds me, Arthur,' Elizabeth Moonlight broke in, 'since we were an odd number tonight I invited that nice Mr Dankton to join us for dinner. He'll be a little late because he's been working and involved in the . . . er . . . goings on. Poor man, Scarbuck appears to drive him so hard, and he was pathetically grateful when I rang.' She turned to Treasure. 'He was here a good deal some months ago helping Arthur go through the diaries, but we've hardly seen him since he came to stay at the Hall.'

Treasure watched Moonlight carefully during this announcement, which was received with a stony expression and no audible comment.

'Oh, what a treat,' cried Miss Goodbody with genuine enthusiasm. 'He's really quite famous, you know, but I haven't found him very approachable. This'll be a marvellous opportunity to pick his brains.'

'Arthur brought him in on the diaries because he'd just discovered a diary kept by Sarah's father in a house they were knocking down in Northampton – didn't you, darling?' Elizabeth realized that her invitation to Dankton had somehow upset her husband. 'Sarah probably got her diary-keeping habit from her father.'

'Yes,' said Moonlight grudgingly, 'I lent Dankton the first few volumes, which seemed to interest him, but the editing I was talking about is being done by a Fellow of Hertford College.'

'And was Sarah really the great patroness of the arts her father said she was?' enquired Miss Goodbody, who was mildly surprised and a little disappointed that Moonlight had never mentioned the existence of the diaries to her.

'In a social-climbing sort of way, yes,' replied Moonlight,

filling her glass from the sherry decanter in his hand. 'But
as for your Shakespeare business, I'm afraid you'll get no
joy from the diaries. All that was well before Sarah's
time.'

'But does she mention any play-acting here?'

'Yes, there's a bit about some masques that Sarah performed in herself; it appears she liked dressing up.'

'And undressing too . . . hee, hee, hee,' squeaked the
Bishop. 'You really ought to read these diaries, Timothy,
they're hot stuff.'

'I imagine one needs a certain familiarity with the script
and the English of the time truly to benefit from the work,'
boomed Mrs Wringle in an evident effort to discourage the
Vicar of Mitchell Stoke from attempting such clearly
corrupting literature.

'You'd think so, but one gets into the swing of it quite
well after a day or two,' Moonlight replied. 'Sarah was
pretty basic in her language.'

'And in her habits too,' put in the Bishop, whose following
peal of laughter was cut short by a stern glance from the
dominant Mrs Wringle.

'Ah, Mr Dankton,' cried Elizabeth Moonlight, looking
towards the door of the drawing-room. She crossed the room,
and taking the arm of the last guest to arrive introduced him
around the assembled party.

It occurred to Trapp and to Treasure simultaneously
that Dankton looked much more the learned bibliographer
and ascetic scholar when free of his artisan's clothing. He
was dressed in a neat black suit, cut in the most current
style, which accentuated both his slimness and his pallor.
The formalities over, he turned to his hostess. 'I do apologize
for being late. I was detained . . . er . . . as it were, by the
police. This ghastly business of the gravedigger – very
upsetting.' He stroked his forehead. 'I'm so sensitive in such
matters.' The rest of the company looked suitably grave –
except for Moonlight who handed Dankton a glass of sherry
with every appearance of regretting this elementary gesture
of hospitality. 'It was, in any event, most kind of you, yes,

most kind to have invited me. There's a dinner – a kind of jamboree, at the Hall this evening. I was not included for reasons best known to Mr Scarbuck. I am not, of course, a member of his group, or organization, or whatever he calls it.'

Dankton did not add that Scarbuck had positively commanded him to accept Lady Moonlight's invitation.

Treasure was anxious for up-to-date news on the police investigation. 'I gather the police have opened the grave,' he said.

'Yes, and closed it again,' replied Dankton without emotion. 'They are now satisfied that the . . . er . . . tragedy could not have taken place there. Their theory is that Mr Worple, whose home is this side of the church, scaled the wall – not the one to the Hall garden – ' he glanced at Trapp – 'but the one to the road, which is lower. They think he fell off it into the road where he was run over by some kind of vehicle.'

'Well, if they believe that they'll believe anything,' said Trapp firmly. 'I mean, why should Worple have climbed the church wall?'

'Unfortunately, in former times he'd have used the Hall gate,' explained Dankton, 'but now, of course, it's locked. The police think he was popping home for a cup of tea – in fact his daughter was expecting him to do so.'

'So he breaks his neck, a car runs over him, the driver thinks he's killed someone, pops the body in the boot, drives to Old Windsor, puts Worple in a boat, and sets fire to him – preposterous!' exclaimed Trapp.

'Put that way, I agree,' said Treasure slowly, 'but that may be something near what actually happened.'

'Only if the driver was potty and perhaps owned that boat-house,' added Miss Goodbody innocently. 'But that wasn't the case because the owner's abroad – the Inspector said so. His name is Colonel Can – something – Wright.'

'Not Freddy Canwath-Wright?' Elizabeth glanced quickly at her husband and then back to Dankton. 'But, Mr Dankton, he's a friend of yours and my husband's as well. What an

absolutely incredible coincidence.' She turned to Treasure.
'It was Freddy who put Mr Dankton in touch with Arthur
over the Northampton diary we were talking about.'

'Well, coincidences do happen, Elizabeth,' answered
Treasure, inwardly wishing he could believe that one had
manifested itself on this occasion.

'Do you know the boat-house, Mr Dankton?' asked
Treasure.

Dankton hesitated. 'I was there once – last summer some
time. I remember it very vaguely. It is a rather embarrassing
coincidence.' He turned to Moonlight. 'Do you know it
yourself, Sir Arthur?' His voice did not register the hope
he felt.

'Didn't even know Freddy kept a boat there; his home's
on the other side of Camberley.' Treasure breathed a sigh
of relief.

'Anyway, the police seem to be transferring their main
investigation from here to Old Windsor,' said Dankton, 'so
they should be leaving us alone for the evening.'

'I wonder if they've found the yellow Volkswagen,'
commented the Bishop looking from side to side brightly.
'Constable Humble came to ask us if we'd seen one just
before we left the cottage this evening.'

Treasure looked across at Dankton who stared straight
back at him steadily before saying, 'They asked me about
that too – that's why I was late. Did anyone here see the
car?'

Treasure decided to volunteer nothing, but Miss Goodbody offered, 'I saw it this afternoon. The policeman who
came to the vicarage asked if I'd noted the number – I wish
I had.'

Both the Bishop and his wife were about to add something but were forestalled by their hostess.

Elizabeth Moonlight had had enough of her currently
least favourite subject. 'Mr Dankton,' she said, 'we were
talking about Sarah Moonlight's diaries just before you came
in. Was she really such a scarlet woman?'

'I'm afraid she was, Lady Moonlight – though she managed

to conceal the fact from both her husband and her father. She left here in some haste during the summer of 1644 to stay with her parents at Corble Manor in Northampton, ostensibly because it was safer, actually because her current and wealthy lover lived nearby. She left there with him for France in August of that year, and if the lover hadn't died of smallpox within a month I doubt she would ever have returned to England.'

'Was he very rich?' enquired Miss Goodbody, who was enjoying the story.

'I could answer that if I knew who he was,' replied Dankton. 'Sarah had an exasperating habit of referring to many of her boy-friends only by their Christian names – this one was called Edward, which offers a wide field for speculation. I'm narrowing it down, though – in between digging swimming pools. He was unmarried and somewhat younger than Sarah.'

'So was Charles the Second,' put in the Bishop. 'Cradlesnatching seems to have been Sarah's speciality.'

'Yes, just as his was married women. She met Charles at The Hague in '48 by which time she was a bit tight for cash,' continued Dankton. 'After that he keeps popping up in the diaries – or rather, she keeps popping up at Court, wherever Charles was running it. It's unfortunate that there are no diaries covering the last two years of the exile. One would like to have known whether she came back in the King's baggage like La Castlemaine.'

'You mean Barbara Palmer, later Lady Castlemaine,' chipped in the Bishop, whose knowledge of the royal intrigues appeared exhaustive. 'After the official junketings on the evening of the Restoration the King slipped over the river to Lambeth and spent the night with her. I've always thought that excessively daring.'

'And curiously irresponsible,' added Mrs Wringle with evident disdain.

'We do know, from the diaries, that Sarah was back here at Mitchell Stoke soon after,' Dankton went on, 'and here she stayed, with money simply pouring in from the King –

though it hardly seems likely he was getting value for it at that stage. Sarah adapted pretty quickly.' He turned to Elizabeth. 'This house was built on what you might call pleasure money, and pleasure was what Sarah encouraged in it for a surprising number of years.'

'Do you suppose the King owed her more than a return for supplying home comforts abroad?' asked Treasure lightly.

'Unlikely, I should have thought,' commented Moonlight. 'As Mr Dankton has explained, she was pretty broke when she met him so it's difficult to imagine how she could have lent or given him money in exile.'

'The missing diaries might explain,' said Elizabeth.

'They aren't necessarily missing, my dear,' said Moonlight. 'It's more than possible they never existed.' Then with hardly a pause he looked across to Trapp and abruptly changed the subject. 'Timothy, I picked up the new lock for the crypt door on my way into Oxford. It fits all right – I started fixing it on when I got back, but I didn't have time to finish. I'll do it tomorrow.'

'That really is kind of you,' replied the Vicar. He turned to Treasure. 'The old latch is broken, and when the door swings open, apart from the eerie creaks, I get wafts of positively refrigerated air in the sanctuary . . . much better to lock the place permanently. Oh, perhaps you'd like to hang on to the key yourself, Sir Arthur?' he added hastily.

'Is the crypt ever used?' asked Treasure.

'No; it's not heated for one thing,' explained Trapp, 'and when the church was wired for electricity they conveniently forgot the crypt. In any case, the place is very small. Children enjoy visiting it, of course . . .'

'And breaking their necks on the stairs,' put in Elizabeth unthinkingly.

'I recall when my father was Vicar . . .' began the Bishop, but before he could begin what Miss Goodbody confidently expected would be a tale of immoral goings-on in the subterranean regions of St John's, Mitchell Stoke, the double doors to the drawing-room were flung wide to reveal Aggie, plump and short, resplendent in starched white cap and apron but swaying slightly from the effort involved in effecting such a dramatic entrance.

'Dinner is served, m'lady,' she cried at the top of her voice, 'but them potatoes 'as gone black.'

CHAPTER XIV

'A crime entirely without motive is very rare indeed . . . in my experience,' observed Chief Inspector Bantree sagely. 'Even vandalism has its motives in rebellion against society . . . Pass the chocolate, there's a good chap.'

Sergeant Wadkin opened the glove box in front of the passenger seat and with difficulty extracted a crumpled chocolate package from behind two fishing reels, a blue rubber bone, several tape cassettes, and a broken breathalyser.

'Help yourself, and break me off a bit,' continued Bantree as he turned the car left on to the main Reading road. 'That's as close to dinner as we'll get tonight. And major crime – murder – has to have a motive behind it.'

'Or a madman?' Wadkin suggested tentatively.

'All right, nut cases excepted,' Bantree agreed. 'But I doubt even a criminally insane person would develop an obsession for knocking off gravediggers. No, there simply has to be a motive; that is, if we're dealing with murder . . . The two-accident theory is perfectly tenable depending on who was involved. If the chap broke his neck falling off the wall into the road, and whoever ran over him panicked because he *thought* he'd killed Worple, then irrational action might have followed.'

'But hardly on quite such an elaborate scale, surely?'

'You mean carting the body all the way to Old Windsor? Well, it seems unlikely, but dumping a corpse on the roadside before lunch on a Saturday between here and Staines wouldn't be all that easy to do unobserved. It'd be like looking for a good picnic spot – you know, the place is never just

right. I agree, though, the boat-house bit – and the fire –
seem a bit excessive. But again, it depends who was involved.
A drunken High Court Judge might take enormous pains
to cover up an accident.' Since a recent acquittal, High Court
Judges came high on Bantree's list of undesirables, which was
why the example he had given was the first to come to mind.
On private reflection he concluded that he had never
actually encountered a drunken judge, and would certainly
not have expected to do so in charge of a car during the fore-
noon on a public road. He took the last piece of chocolate
proffered by Wadkin. 'All sorts of important people behave
out of character if they find themselves on the wrong side
of the law – politicians, actors, diplomats – even policemen,'
he added to prove his lack of prejudice.

'But if the chap ran over Worple without anyone seeing –
and nobody seems to have – why did he trouble to stop and
pick up the body? Why didn't he just drive on?'

'Ah, that rather makes my point. If the driver was a normally responsible person he'd stop to see if the victim was
dead . . .'

'And having discovered he was dead, wouldn't he just
get back in the car and drive like hell – assuming there were
still no witnesses?'

'The theory just doesn't stand up, does it?' said Bantree,
whose theory it had been in the first place. 'But if Worple
didn't fall off the wall, where did he die? If he fell into the
grave he'd dug, he wouldn't have been so badly injured –
and who fished him out? And if someone did, and then carted
the body across the churchyard to the main gate – ' he paused
– 'or to the vicarage, all unseen . . . The Vicar was at the
Dower House, wasn't he?'

'Yes, sir, but Banquet's wife – the Vicar's housekeeper –
says she was cleaning the windows at the front of the house
between ten-thirty and twelve – so she'd have seen a car or
van if one had been in the drive.'

'The gate to the Hall was locked, so unless Mr Eustace
Dankton is lying in his teeth, and risking being given away
when we get that interpreter, nobody trundled a body out

that way. Incidentally, we've learned something today –
Filipinos from Mindanao don't speak Filipino; they speak
Sulu. Remember that, Sergeant, it may prove to be of in-
estimable value to you in the future.'

'I should think that depends on whether the Home Office
allows Mr Scarbuck to import any more tourists,' Wadkin
replied with a grin.

'I can tell you, Mr Griffith Speke-Jones, MP, back-
pedalled on that one pretty swiftly. He has no business
connection with Scarbuck whatsoever – or so he says. The
only interest he's shown so far was in finding out whether
there's been a Press release on the murder. I told him we're
instructed to treat it as an accident until the morning – he
nearly collapsed with relief. He'll be off tonight or at the
crack of dawn, well ahead of the gentlemen from the Press –
you see. Anyway, we can do without politicians in this or
any other case. They always behave like Chief Constables –
even the guilty ones.'

'The rain was now falling more heavily. Bantree leant
forward in the driving seat as they drove through a huge
pool of water on the road. He switched on the windscreen
wipers to double speed.

'I must let you try some of my last year's Liebfraumilch-
type wine, Sergeant. Like wine, do you?'

'Oh yes, sir; thank you very much.' Wadkin tried to
sound enthusiastic.

'This home-brewed stuff is an acquired taste, of course.
My wife says it's all right if you don't smell it – if you don't
breathe in while you're drinking . . . As a matter of fact,
she's right.' The car hit another large puddle at speed.

'If this keeps up, Mr Scarbuck's swimming pool will be
ready for use in the morning.' The Inspector was concentrating on the driving and made no reply. 'I haven't met
the banker yet, sir; is he all right?'

'Merchant banker – very special breed; effortless superio-
rity. He's switched on, though; been playing games with me
all day, but only because he thought his noble relation might
be involved in the murder . . . which is curious when you

think about it. Why should Treasure think Sir Arthur Moonlight's been doing in a gravedigger? That's why he didn't tell me this story about the pugnacious pansy earlier. At first I thought he'd made it up – bloody cat.' Bantree swerved to avoid the animal. 'He's straight, of course – just prudent about taking policemen into his confidence until he's ready . . . and careful to keep his friends out of trouble.'

'Mr Scarbuck seemed pretty anxious to keep Forward Britain out of the picture, sir.'

'Yes, private armies don't like holding field days in public. And some of those trade unionists there won't want their photos in the *Mirror* either – living it up at country house parties doesn't go down well with the brothers. There'll be some hide and seek going on tomorrow . . . Now what was the name of the house?'

'The Bishop wasn't sure, sir, but the location and description's quite clear. It should be about half a mile on from here – double white gates on the river side, For Sale notice, steep drive down to a thatched cottage with a tall chimney – his wife never even noticed the car.'

'You don't if you're driving.' Bantree slowed the Ford to a crawl. 'Anyway it was still pretty observant of the Bishop to remember all that . . .'

'Here it is,' Wadkin interrupted. 'A steep and very rutted drive by the look of it, sir.'

'And no compensation if I write off the underside of my car either,' said Bantree, surveying the plunging, broken surface that began a few feet ahead of his front wheels. 'Let this be a lesson to you, Sergeant: never plan to go fishing straight from duty.' Since Wadkin neither fished nor owned a private car, this homily was wasted. Bantree was now regretting the decision not to have made this particular journey in the police car they had left behind at Mitchell Stoke.

'Those tulips are early,' remarked the Inspector to take his mind off the way the vehicle was slipping and swaying 'I've often thought of getting plastic ones for sticking in at Easter – surprise for the neighbours. Right, we're down.'

He drew up outside the front door of a well-kept, white-washed cottage of considerable age and charm. Despite the narrowness and disrepair of the approach the drive widened into a reasonably large and even forecourt, level with the house. 'Well, at least we shan't have to back out.' Bantree switched off the engine.

'And there's our yellow Volkswagen.' Wadkin pointed to an open garage door.

'Well done the Bishop. Now if this were an American TV film we should draw our guns, take up positions on either side of the door prior to your kicking it in. Have you ever kicked in a front door?'

'No, sir.'

'Well, don't try – it's a terrible strain on the ankles. Since we're in Berkshire, let's just ring the bell and see what happens. But remember, we may be interviewing a murderer with curious propensities – so mind my back.'

'It wasn't bad grub,' said Scarbuck to Speke-Jones as they mounted the stairs of the Hall. 'Outside caterers of course, four pounds a head excluding wine.' The two had enough in common where values were concerned for Speke-Jones automatically to begin a mental calculation. 'Anyroad, they'll be happy enough in the saloon for a bit. There's plenty of port going round.'

'What is it you want a word about?' asked Speke-Jones. 'I don't think we should be away too long.'

'Let's go in here.' Scarbuck opened the door on a room half-furnished as an office at the head of the stairway. 'This'll be one of the new bathrooms.' Speke-Jones was tired of being treated to the grand tour of Mitchell Hall, and showed it. 'Sit down a minute, Griffith,' said Scarbuck ingratiatingly, and, motioning towards the more comfortable of the two chairs in the room, took the other, behind a desk, himself. 'About this little matter of Movement funds . . .'

'It's not so little, and my view hasn't altered.' Speke-Jones spoke sternly and to the point. 'You've handled this whole business in a way that can only be described as cavalier.

Now either you turn over Forward Britain Enterprises to the Movement on Monday, or you can bloody well sweat it out.'

'But, Griffith, lad, they're practically one and the same already. I've only the best interests of the Movement at heart,' Scarbuck attempted to look hurt. 'You know my reasoning, and you've no more faith in the judgement of the other officers than I have. A word from you now and they'd all agree to transfer the half million straight away. I'll have the collateral tomorrow morning in any case.'

'Well, there's two little "ifs" to be put in there. If you have the collateral tomorrow,' corrected Speke-Jones, 'then you can find out on Monday if you have the title to it.'

'But where's the doubt? This place is mine . . . that's to say ours, and everything in it is ours. The deed of sale has a special clause stating just that.'

'You were right the first time, George. This place is yours – not ours – because Enterprises is yours. And a nice scandal there's going to be on Tuesday when the City finds out how you've funded it. I told you right at the start the Movement should have bought Mitchell Hall in its own right, and it can buy it from you on Monday for half a million if you're willing, and that's more than double what you paid. We'll want all the assets, of course.'

'And how much good will it do the Movement if the President is done for misapprehension of funds, I'd like to know? Have you asked yourself that?'

Speke-Jones gave a half-smile. 'Yes, George, I've asked myself that, and I've come up with the same answer since you got a murder on your hands as I did before you acquired such a foolish complication – only now the answer's a bit firmer, that's all. You know, George, I've never believed you made a very suitable President. But don't worry, you won't go to jail – not for misappropriation anyway. Following your resignation – ' he paused to ensure that the meaning of his words was being properly digested – 'I repeat, following your resignation from the Movement, and from Enterprises, we shall, of course, be very ready publicly to announce our willingness to take over the company and to meet all its obligations. Indeed, we shall recognize our moral responsibility in the matter. I don't believe the Movement will suffer – on the contrary.'

This was too much for Scarbuck. 'You rotten Welsh bast . . .'

'Language, George, language, and watch it or you'll have the Race Relations on to you too.' Speke-Jones was as cool and in command of himself and the situation as Scarbuck was outraged.

'So that's what you want – the Presidency. After all my years of unmilitated effort, taking a mere idea and nursing it through thick and thin . . .'

'Save me the violin music, there's a good chap. You've done well, George, no doubt about it, and the Movement will be sorry to see you go. But it's too big for you now; there's too much at stake. Go back to building hospitals and posh flats – you're good at that. Mind you, whether you go back a respected member of the community or with the old image a bit tarnished like . . . well, that's entirely up to you. Write me a letter of resignation which we can show to all those nice people downstairs and your problems are over. And calm down or you'll burst a blood vessel.'

Scarbuck did appear to be on the point of apoplexy. He loosened his collar and dabbed his forehead with a handkerchief, breathing heavily the while. He also took the opportunity to consider a new strategy. 'All right, Griffith, you win,' he said in a tone of too abject surrender, 'but there's a better way open for you personally – and you can take it if you'll leave me the Presidency.' Speke-Jones remained poker-faced. 'I'll assign you half the shares in Enterprises, and I'll do it now. How about that?' Scarbuck leant back with a look of confident triumph.

Speke-Jones shook his head. 'There was a time, George, when I should have considered that offer magnanimous in the extreme – yes indeed. Coming at this moment, though, it falls a bit flat to say the least. D'you see, it's not just the money I'm after, and in any case why should I settle for half of three million when I can control everything from Tuesday?'

'Ay, well that's where you're wrong. In the first place controlling the funds of the Movement through the Presidency isn't the same as owning them – if I'd thought it was I'd not have troubled to set up Enterprises. In the second place there won't be three million. I've agreed from the start that Dankton and what he calls his partners will get a quarter of what's realized – and if he wasn't such a damn fool he'd have stuck out for more. Well, you can't pay Dankton out through the Movement's funds – there is a Constitution, you know, drawn up by proper lawyers . . .'

'And in the third place,' Speke-Jones interrupted, 'there's no three million yet because there's no manuscript yet – but there's two million in the Movement's balances, and I'll settle for that even if your expensive treasure hunt turns into a wild goose chase.'

'There's a manuscript all right – Dankton's certain of that – and it'll fetch a bloody sight more than three million if it's allowed out of the country – that library in America . . .'

'It won't be allowed out of the country, George, so you can forget the Pierpont Morgan Library and all your other Yankee prospects – it'd be like selling the Crown Jewels to the Arabs. Parliament would never allow it.' Speke-Jones didn't stop to consider whether his analogy was altogether a sound one in view of the country's economic state.

Scarbuck was not concerned with fine points. 'You mean *you* as a Member of Parliament – God help us – would oppose it?'

Speke-Jones ignored the insult. 'As a Member of Parliament and as President of Forward Britain I'd oppose it. The Movement would collect enormous kudos in the process. I've even considered giving the manuscript to the British Museum.'

This remark brought Scarbuck to the verge of tears. 'Nay, lad, you wouldn't do that . . . you couldn't do that?' The dismay was genuine.

'No, George, I shan't do that. I said I'd considered the

matter, but on reflection I think it only proper that all parties concerned should benefit along with the nation. The manuscript will go for auction with a modest reserve, and out of the proceeds the Movement will graciously – and quite constitutionally – reward the learned Mr Dankton, and also Sir Arthur Moonlight, with generous *ex gratia* payments. There may even be a bit for you, George. That way, everything's neat and above board. The Movement will keep most of the money, of course, but there'll be no hard feelings, plenty of goodwill, and – who knows – perhaps a bit of public recognition for yours truly.'

'A knighthood?' Scarbuck's lip curled as he uttered the words.

'Possibly – possibly not; who knows? In any event the Forward Britain Movement will come out of it very well, with enough funds to pay for all its new cultural and socially beneficial programmes.'

'What programmes?' enquired the current President.

'You may well ask, George, after all the hot air you've been spouting today. Proper programmes, boyo, that will get the Movement integrated into the political, industrial and educational structures of this country – and in a way you couldn't envision if you devoted yourself to the subject for the next hundred years. You're too narrow, George; despite all the flim-flam, you're a money grabber at heart, and you'll never be anything else . . . Now let's have this resignation written out straight away, there's a good fellow.'

CHAPTER XV

The Bishop was seated on Elizabeth Moonlight's right. He gazed with interest, and no apparent surprise, at the empty plate Aggie had just placed before him, and then at the piece of lemon meringue pie which she had neatly tipped off it into his table napkin. 'There's many a slip twixt cup and lip,' he exclaimed with a giggle. The Bishop had eaten well and drunk better. 'I'm not supposed to have pudding, but since this is gift-wrapped already, perhaps I might take it home for tomorrow's tea?'

'Aggie, the Bishop's dessert!' cried the embarrassed hostess.

''E's got one,' replied Aggie defensively as she continued to circle the round table, balancing a tray of plates with the defiant air of an amateur conjuror about to attempt the impossible. She glanced back at the Bishop's empty plate in amazement. 'Sorry, your Lordship,' she exclaimed, swinging back with such alacrity that only gravity served to keep the contents of the tray intact. 'Could of sworn I give you some.'

Despite this minor disaster, dinner had been a success if a somewhat prolonged affair due to the eccentricities of the service. Thelma Goodbody, seated between Bishop Wringle and Eustace Dankton, had been taking full advantage of the opportunity to acquire both local and expert knowledge for her research project. Moonlight, with Mrs Wringle on his right, had been carefully isolated from Dankton by Elizabeth. She had placed Trapp between her husband and the bibliographer for whom Moonlight appeared to have developed a hardly concealed aversion.

The problem of the Bishop's dessert overcome, Treasure, who was on Elizabeth's left, diplomatically returned to an earlier topic. 'So *As You Like It* is still a runner for Mitchell Stoke, Thelma?'

'The Bishop's more encouraging than Mr Dankton,' replied Miss Goodbody.

'And, alas, more lacking in scholarship,' put in the Bishop modestly. 'Bardolatry is no substitute for learning. I sincerely hope Shakespeare may have visited this place, so naturally I make too much of the purely circumstantial evidence that exists to suggest he did.' He gazed benignly around the table. 'There are Arden Cottages all over England, though the pair in the village here were certainly so named in 1640 – perhaps after the setting of *As You Like It* in Arden Forest; perhaps even by an occupant who saw the play – perhaps by chance.' He uttered a loud hiccough, said, 'I beg your pardon,' to Elizabeth, and uttered another one.

'They were almost certainly built from stone salvaged from the old Hall in the sixteen-thirties,' offered Moonlight from across the table.

'With carpentry supplied by Jaques Snate or Snathe – one of the three sons born to John and Mary Snathe in May 1599,' added Miss Goodbody. She turned to Dankton. 'Sir Arthur has an account for nineteen shillings and eight pence to prove it.'

'Probably expensive joinery for labourers' cottages in those days,' said Moonlight. 'We gave all the accounts for the building of this house to the Soane Museum, and Sarah Moonlight appears to have been tighter-fisted with tradesmen and artisans than her husband thirty years before.'

'Living as an exile in reduced circumstances probably induced that habit,' put in Dankton primly, with the air of one who had suffered poverty in his time. 'I must admit I'm more sceptical about the cottages than the naming of the carpenter's awful children, which does seem uncannily coincidental. The problem is that the play could as easily have been written in 1593 as 1599 – as Miss Goodbody is well aware, and if Shakespeare himself came with the players to a lesser country house – forgive me, Sir Arthur – the earlier year is a better bet than the later. A lot of the companies went on the road in '92 and '93 because of the plague in London.'

'But Shakespeare did *As You Like It* at Wilton in 1603 and probably in the three preceding years,' said Miss Goodbody firmly. 'There's a letter to prove it.'

'It's alleged there was once a letter at Wilton to prove it – since mysteriously disappeared,' corrected Dankton, 'but the 1603 performance was in the presence of the King, and the playwright of the King's Players would have made the effort to take part in a command performance. I doubt Shakespeare came here first for a dry run four years in advance.'

Treasure felt his protégée was being put down too easily. 'There is the point that this particular play was eminently suited for performing in country house gardens,' he said, though he had only Miss Goodbody's word on the subject.

'A very slim point, I'm afraid,' replied Dankton. 'The performances at Wilton always took place in December, which hardly suggests they were done outdoors. It's true, though, that *As You Like It* was a favourite on what was called the "mansion circuit". It wasn't all that popular in London – Touchstone the clown wasn't considered a patch on Sir Toby.'

The Bishop carefully examined his empty wine glass. 'I was brought up to the notion that the play belonged to the high fanatical . . .' he tried again . . . 'the high fantastical period of Shakespeare's work. Doesn't that suggest it was written after 1598?'

'Re-written,' said Miss Goodbody, conscious that as the putative principal in this discussion her contribution so far had been somewhat meagre. 'There's a theory, tied up with the death of Marlowe, that Shakespeare began to write the play in blank verse during 1593, abandoned it, and then dusted it off again six years later. It's easy to separate the verse-form bits from the straight prose when you read the play.'

'There were an unusual number of live births recorded in the parish around January 1600,' put in the Bishop. Several of those present construed that this gratuitous irrelevance was the result of too much drink. As if sensing this, he went on, 'The fact is highly pertinent,' and, pausing only to suppress a hiccough, continued: 'It suggests the very probable conclusion of a visit to a lonely country village of an all male troupe of roguish players in the er . . . in the merry month of May! Just imagine the effect on the village maidens. Mmm . . . I do stress also that the births were live, which suggests the infusion of new . . . er . . . blood into the community. Too much inter-marriage and even . . . er . . . incestuous relationships, were the cause of infant mortality in closed communities in those days. One saw the same thing in Africa in quite recent times.'

The only other person present who might have confirmed the last unsavoury fact, to wit Mrs Wringle, made no move to do so. On the contrary, the Bishop's consort had been treating him to censorious glances throughout his soliloquy, evidently to indicate that an assessment of the relative fertility of pliant maidens, whether in rural England or backward Africa, was no fit subject for the dinner table.

In contrast, Miss Goodbody was delighted with such intelligences. 'What a super theory. Whoever loved that loved not at first sight,' she cried triumphantly, clasping the Bishop's right hand. 'Timothy, did you know about the population explosion here at the beginning of 1600?'

'No, I didn't,' replied the Vicar, 'but the Bishop's much better at deciphering the old registers than I am. I suppose tomorrow you'll be searching them for more Jaques and Orlandos.'

'And don't forget the Rosalinds,' added Dankton archly. 'Those boy players appear to have thrived on country air.'

Treasure noted that this single light aside was the only fresh indication from Dankton that Thelma Goodbody's theory might have substance. Since Dankton, in her own words, had first set Thelma on the trail she was following, Treasure found it incongruous that the bibliographer seemed now to be pouring cold water on all the girl's conclusions. Nor could he have been aware that Dankton was present at Elizabeth Moonlight's table for the express purpose of establishing at that time his own scholarly disbelief in the theory that Shakespeare ever graced Mitchell Stoke with his presence.

Mrs Wringle studied her wristwatch with some ceremony. 'Forgive us, Elizabeth, I think we ought to be going. It's well past Clarence's bedtime.' There was no refuting this statement since the Bishop had suddenly gone to sleep, holding Miss Goodbody's hand; the full coffee cup before him was the only container for liquid he had left undrained during the course of the meal.

There followed a general movement away from the table and into the hall, with more comment about the lateness of the hour from Trapp, who had an early morning service in mind, and from Thelma Goodbody, who was relying on

Trapp to transport her across the Thames on the chain ferry – the mechanics of which did not invite manipulation by a lady in evening dress.

'The rain's stopped,' observed Moonlight from the porch after seeing off the Wringles in their dilapidated Mini. Dankton had already disappeared into the night. 'I'll walk down to the ferry with you both – and we'll go through the churchyard. I've got a key to that wretched gate, and Timothy can protect us from marauders,' he added lightly.

'Good evening, sir, sorry to disturb you at this hour,' said Chief Inspector Bantree. Treasure had answered the door bell after emerging from the kitchen of the Dower House. He had been dutifully assisting Elizabeth in doing those things that Aggie had left undone before retiring. 'I wonder if we might come in for a moment?'

'Certainly, Inspector. I'm afraid Sir Arthur is out, but he should be back soon.' Treasure opened the door wider.

'That's all right, sir, it's you we've really come to see.' But Treasure hardly heard the words. His attention was fixed not upon Bantree nor Sergeant Wadkin, but on the equally familiar figure that entered the hall with them. The tousled, blond hair was now brushed and neat. The casual, blue jean suit and jewellery were not in evidence, for the man was dressed in a black gaberdine raincoat, of good quality, buttoned at the top. His trousers and shoes were also black. He wore thickly framed spectacles which added to his studious, respectable appearance. Yet there was no mistaking the man who had so abruptly barred Treasure's way that afternoon, and then subjected him to dire threats.

'This is a little unusual, sir, even a bit irregular, but in the circumstances . . .' The Inspector hesitated because of Treasure's astonished expression. 'Do you recognize this gentleman, sir?'

'I certainly do, Inspector – and I shall be extremely surprised if he doesn't recognize me.'

'No question about it,' opened the man in black with a smile. 'This is the gentleman I spoke with across from the Hall earlier today. Nice to get properly acquainted, Mr Treasure sir, my name's Happenwack – sounds kinda funny I know, but that's what it is, Dale Henry Happenwack.'

Treasure was positive he recognized the man, yet the clothes, the bearing, and above all, the distinctly American accent were completely out of character. Happenwack continued to smile as he undid his coat to reveal a clerical collar and black stock.

'We called on the Reverend Happenwack earlier this evening, sir. He immediately confirmed having met you. Indeed he's been to Mitchell Stoke twice today . . .'

'Sure,' Happenwack interrupted the Inspector. 'I was hoping to catch up with the Rector, or Vicar, is it? Guess I ran out of luck, though. He wasn't at the clergy house mid-morning, and, as Mr Treasure himself told me, he had a burial service going on when I called round after lunch.'

'I told you the Vicar was conducting a service?' Treasure asked incredulously.

'Why yes, sir,' replied Happenwack earnestly, 'don't you remember? I explained I was staying nearby and wondered whether I could help with services tomorrow. I'm an Episcopalian.' He turned to the Inspector. 'That's the same as Church of England back home.'

Treasure considered and dismissed the possibility he was suffering from delusions. The man before him was certainly a liar and probably an impostor. He decided the inevitable exposure should take a logical order, at least for the benefit of the policemen. 'Has Mr Happenwack told you how he was dressed when we met, Inspector?'

'Yes, sir, and the description of his clothing tallies exactly with the one you gave us.'

'Gee, come to that I guess I did look a little unpriestly,' put in Happenwack. 'You see, Mr Treasure, I'm here rubber-necking around Oxford and the churches in the locality, which is why I was dressed for comfort.'

'Mr Happenwack has a furnished cottage just the other side of Pangbourne, sir,' said Bantree.

'Has Mr Happenwack told you what he said to me this

afternoon, Inspector?'

'Yes, sir, and that's the problem. The account you gave of the conversation and the one Mr Happenwack gives just don't tie up . . .'

'Conversation!' exclaimed Treasure. 'There was no conversation. This man treated me to a series of threats and left me speechless.'

'Heck, Mr Treasure, I don't know what you're talking about,' said Happenwack with wide-eyed innocence. 'I asked you about the Vicar, you told me about the service, and that was it. I didn't threaten you, sir; I'd never seen you before; I didn't know who you were; why should I have threatened you? I didn't threaten the lady at the clergy house or the gentleman I met at the Hall this morning.'

'That's true, sir,' Bantree confirmed. 'When Mr Happenwack was here this morning, he spoke with Mrs Banquet at the vicarage and also with Mr Dankton. We've interviewed both parties — Mr Dankton just a few minutes ago — and both confirm that Mr Happenwack was simply enquiring about the Vicar.'

'So what possible explanation is there for my having told you that Mr Happenwack, as he calls himself, threatened me?'

'That's precisely what we were wondering, sir. Could it be you're confusing Mr Happenwack with someone else . . . er . . .'

'Oh, come off it, Inspector, either I've told you a pack of lies or else this man is lying.'

'Yes, sir.' The Inspector's tone was noncommittal.

Treasure swallowed firmly to suppress his anger. He tried as coolly as possible to see the situation from the policeman's viewpoint. Here were two men offering entirely different versions of the encounter that both admitted had taken place. One of the men was a priest — or purported to be one — the other was, dammit, an affluent merchant banker; God and mammon personified. Faced with the kind of dilemma now confronting the Inspector, Treasure realized how he himself would react. He also recalled the coolness in

Bantree's manner when, before dinner, he had listened to Treasure's account of what had taken place – an account overdue by the three hours that had elapsed since their first meeting outside the vicarage. Treasure fought to suppress the sweat he felt breaking out on his forehead. If Bantree had found his delayed story of the episode fishy when he had first heard it, what was he thinking now: probably that the whole thing had been cooked up to draw suspicion away from the Moonlights. But the situation was preposterous. Treasure knew that he, Treasure, was telling the truth – somehow he had to prove it by discrediting the all too credible Happenwack.

'Inspector, how do you know Mr Happenwack is who he says he is?'

'A very proper question in the circumstances, sir, though we already have the answer. We've been in touch with the American Embassy, sir. Mr Happenwack is listed in the Episcopal Church register as assistant priest at the church of St John the Divine, Roundtop, Westchester County, New York State. His passport is in order, and he arrived here two weeks ago.'

'You did say Roundtop, Inspector?' The policeman nodded as Treasure went on. 'Does Mr Happenwack have friends here, anyone who can confirm his identity?'

'Not exactly, sir . . .'

Happenwack intervened. 'Heck, Mr Treasure, I'm a tourist. I've saved up for three years to make this trip. I've never been to this country before. No, I don't have friends here – why should I have, but why should I tell lies?'

'And you deny having told me about an accident?'

'What's there to deny? I don't know of any accident. The Inspector here tells me there's been what sounds like a murder – and that's a very shocking thing – but if I knew anything about an accident or a murder I guess I'd have told the police.'

Treasure was conscious that Bantree and Wadkin were content with being silent observers of this interchange. 'Mr Happenwack, who is Stacey?' he asked quietly.

'The Inspector already asked me that one, and as far as I know she's a figment of your imagination, sir.'

'She?'

'Well, the only Staceys I know are girls – but they're all back in the States.' Happenwack glanced around the group. 'Isn't Stacey a girl's name over here?'

'It's not a common name in this country, Mr Happenwack,' offered Bantree.

Treasure sighed. 'So you're not involved in any fifty-fifty deal with a Stacey?'

Happenwack shrugged his shoulders and directed a look of blank incomprehension at the Inspector. The question remained unanswered.

'Assuming Mr Happenwack admits he's been tearing around this village in a yellow Volkswagen, is the car his?' Treasure addressed this question to the Inspector.

'He does admit driving the car, sir, and it belongs to the owner of the cottage Mr Happenwack is renting. The estate agent acting for the owner confirms that the car goes with the cottage. Sergeant Wadkin talked to the gentleman concerned in person an hour ago. The lease was arranged last week – references were waived in view of Mr Happenwack's . . . er . . . profession, though he does have impressive letters of introduction from church dignitaries in America.' The Inspector paused, looking from Treasure to Happenwack, and back again; neither appeared to have anything to say. 'There were, of course, no witnesses to this . . . er . . . conversation, sir?'

The question had been directed at Treasure, but it was Happenwack who replied. 'No, worse luck, and I'm the foreigner so I guess if there's any doubt, I don't get the benefit.'

In some unaccountable way this remark hurt Treasure almost as much as the challenge to his own verity. 'In that supposition, Mr Happenwack,' he said stonily, 'you are entirely wrong. Were it not for the complete impartiality of the British legal system your situation at this moment would be a good deal more uncomfortable than it is.'

In the unlikely event that Happenwack was a priest, Treasure felt that he had missed his true vocation as an actor. The performance was flawless. He also came to the conclusion that it was purposeless to continue the interview. 'Inspector, if it's all the same to you I'd like to go to bed. I appreciate your problem, but you'll accept that it's your problem and not mine. I've told you all I know. Mr Happenwack has given you his version. As I see it, you have to use your own judgement on who is telling the truth. I have no doubt Mr Happenwack has accounted for his movements during today, just as he has satisfied you on the matter of his credentials.' The Inspector nodded, and made as if to say something, but Treasure continued, 'That being the case, I wish you a very good night.'

The vice-chairman of Grenwood, Phipps was unused to having his word questioned, and to suffering the further indignity of having its reliability debated. Equally he did not intend to allow any provincial policeman to get away with false precedents in either context. A plan had formulated in his mind, triggered by a piece of information supplied by the Inspector, and the sooner he could be rid of the present company the sooner he could begin to execute it. Time was of the essence, and the time in New York was six-thirty in the evening.

CHAPTER XVI

'And how's it going to sound when I say I spent the night with the Vicar?' asked Miss Goodbody primly but a shade more lightly than she would have posed the same question when cold sober. The steady flow of wine at dinner had induced a liberalizing euphoria which she was finding entirely agreeable.

'I should say that would depend upon the Vicar,' said Trapp with mock solemnity. 'D'you want some more coffee?'

The two were seated in separate armchairs in the living-

room of the vicarage. Miss Goodbody had eschewed the sofa
– but only just – and was curled up comfortably, shoes discarded as an act of conscious abandonment. Trapp was
sprawled opposite her, absent-mindedly stroking Bach's
head while the recipient of his favours dribbled contentedly
on to his master's best pair of trousers.

Moonlight had found the evening air chilly and had
excused himself to return to the Dower House before the
three had reached the river. Trapp and Miss Goodbody had
later discovered that the chain ferry – a large punt attached to
a submerged length of continuous chain – was moored and
secured on the opposite bank of the river. They had returned
to the vicarage intending to telephone the landlord of The
Jolly Boatman with the request that he unlock the ferry.
This plan had been abandoned after they had come to assess
the degree of jollity likely to be displayed by even the best-
tempered of boatmen summoned from bed at a quarter to
midnight. It was then that Trapp had suggested Miss
Goodbody should sleep at the vicarage.

The girl declined the offer of more coffee, and avoided the
sobering gaze of Bach, who, in the manner of his breed, was
affecting the expression of a not entirely approving elder
statesman. In truth he was simply rather sleepy but unwilling
to miss the bonus of unaccustomed human attention at so
late an hour.

'I can hardly attend eight o'clock Communion dressed
like this.'

'Oh, I don't know, you might set a trend, and anyway,
I think you look rather fetching.' Miss Goodbody wished she
had chosen the sofa after all.

'I suppose I could pop back to The Boatman early and
change. Geoffrey said he'd be here at ten to look at the picture.
I hope the newspaper works.' Miss Goodbody's curator
friend, though frankly sceptical about the provenance of the
painting, had advised spreading newspaper on the treated
part to sop up any residue of white spirit.

'If you intend creeping away from my vicarage in evening
dress at seven o'clock in the morning, I'll be able to sell

tickets for Matins. Tell you what, I'll give you a hand-bell
to ring when you go down the drive!'

Miss Goodbody looked genuinely concerned. 'Timothy,
I think you should take me back in the car.'

'What, and have Constable Humble apprehend me for
driving under the influence?'

'You're not under the influence.'

'Yes, I am – yours . . . Thelma, will you marry me?'

'Timothy, are you serious?'

'I've never been more serious in my life.'

'You're sure you're not a tiny bit tipsy . . . I mean, you
don't look serious.'

Bach was following this exchange like a spectator at a
tennis match with a stiff neck, his eyes moved from Trapp to
Miss Goodbody, and back again, but his head continued to
rest on Trapp's knee.

'Thelma, will you marry me?' repeated Trapp slowly
and distinctly.

Her euphoria increasing to something approaching sheer
ecstasy, the girl rose from the armchair and progressed
shoeless but with dignity to the sofa. Thelma Goodbody
was a romantic at heart. This was her moment, and she did
not intend to have the memory of it spoiled by the confines
of an armchair. Arranging herself in the centre of the sofa
in a pose she considered suitable for the acceptance of a
proposal of marriage – as well as for whatever it was that
came after – she smiled demurely at Trapp. 'Come here and
I'll tell you.'

The answer Miss Goodbody gave Timothy Trapp, bringing contentment to him, (as it did later to his mentor the
Bishop of Oxford) should have marked the end of a perfect
evening.

Mark Treasure waited patiently in the study of the Dower
House, the telephone held close to his ear. Transatlantic
'phone calls were common enough events in his business
life but he had never broken the habit of listening harder
and talking louder on intercontinental telephone lines. The

stage-doorman at the Grant Theater on West 43rd Street, New York, had evinced no particular surprise at receiving a call for Miss Forbes all the way from England. Yes, Miss Forbes was in the theatre but she was not in her dressing-room; 'curtain up' was in fifteen minutes so he guessed she must be around somewhere. If Mr Treasure would hold his horses the call-boy should locate her any minute now.

'Mark, darling, are you all right?'

Treasure assured his wife that the accident, illness, fire, or comparable dire event she invariably assumed preceded a long-distance telephone call from him had been staved off once again. There then followed the familiar endearments, the explanation that he was not in Kuwait but staying with the Moonlights, and his promise to transmit messages of affection to Arthur and Elizabeth.

'Molly, are you going up to Alan and Jill's at Roundtop tonight?' Alan Foster, an expatriate English actor, was in the cast of another Broadway play. He and his wife were old friends of the Treasures, and Molly spent most of her week-ends with them at their home in New York State when she was playing in New York.

'Yes, Alan's picking me up after the show.'

'Good, I want you to do something for me on the way. There's an Episcopalian church in Roundtop called St John the Divine, at least I think there is . . .'

A few minutes later Treasure replaced the telephone with the largest sense of achievement he had experienced all day. If the Reverend Dale Henry Happenwack had wanted to provide Treasure with an open opportunity to check on his background and origins he could hardly have done a better job. Roundtop might have no particular significance for Inspector Bantree, nor would it have had for the vast majority of serving officers in the police forces of Great Britain. It so happened, however, that Molly Forbes, the actress wife of Mark Treasure, was currently spending most of her week-ends there.

Treasure looked at his watch. It was close to midnight, and the return call he had arranged with Molly would come through at any time after five-thirty in the morning. He wanted to be back then in the study to receive it instantly and to avoid the sound of the bell waking the whole household. There were three telephone receivers in the Dower House – the one beside him, another in the kitchen, and the third in Moonlight's dressing-room. Treasure knew that this last instrument was fitted with a 'bell off' switch, a civilizing device provided by the Post Office for those subscribers who, like Treasure himself, preferred to exercise an option on whether or not to have their slumbers disturbed by insomniac friends in the middle of the night. Since Moonlight had no doubt returned from seeing Thelma Goodbody properly launched, Treasure thoughtfully determined to caution his host about silencing his telephone unless he needed rousing at five-thirty.

Treasure ascended the stairs and gave a gentle tap on Moonlight's door. Elizabeth had retired some time before in the main bedroom. Her husband's dressing-room, next door, was fairly large, and big enough to accommodate a bed of its own. Moonlight, who was an asthmatic, generally slept here to avoid disturbing his wife. Treasure opened the door quietly. The room was in darkness, but the light from the hall was sufficient to reveal that the bed was unoccupied. Assuming either that Moonlight had not yet returned or – more likely – that he had joined Elizabeth in the next room, Treasure switched on the light and made for the telephone.

The instrument was on a small table beside the bed. Alongside the 'phone were the books Treasure remembered Moonlight had been carrying when he left the study earlier in the evening. On top of these were two calf-bound volumes of obvious antiquity, and some typed pages. Had the top page been a letter, Treasure would automatically have resisted every temptation to read it. He was conscious as he scanned the heading to the typescript of what was obviously a series of notes that even this action was morally indefensible – but a name and some dates made it somehow compulsive. SARAH MOONLIGHT DIARIES 1658–1659 read the heading. Yet just over an hour before Arthur Moonlight had positively asserted there were no diaries covering those two years.

Adequately to explain or justify what followed, it must be remembered that Treasure had arrived at Mitchell Stoke to discover that one of his nearest friends was not only in a fit of deep depression but also irrationally eager to enter into financial negotiations that, if completed, would reduce him to a state of near penury. He, Treasure, had thereafter spent an anguished afternoon fearful that Moonlight might somehow be involved in – or, at best, caught up in – an act of murder, and just as Moonlight had assuaged concern on this score, he had set up a new train of doubt by virtually admitting he knew more about the demise of Maggie Edwards than he had been prepared to tell his guest. Then there was the smaller but significant point of Moonlight's attitude towards Dankton throughout dinner: he had been close to contemptuous – behaviour on his part that Treasure knew was totally out of character. And despite his own invidious position in relation to the Happenwack affair, Treasure was convinced that any continuing suspicion harboured by Inspector Bantree was based on the belief that he, Treasure, was somehow engaged in protecting Moonlight. There was now evidence in front of Treasure that Moonlight had told a deliberate lie at dinner, and embellished it for his own wife's consumption.

In short, Treasure was close to the belief that Moonlight was so deeply affected by some unhappy event or circumstance as not to be responsible for at least some of his own actions, and it was the summation of these events and conclusions that, occurring to Treasure at this moment, prompted his immediate and some equally important later actions. If the decision to pick up and read the notes on Sarah Moonlight's diaries was prompted through a victory for intuition over a distress of conscience, it was a decision that Treasure never regretted, and one for which Moonlight was to be eternally grateful.

The report read:

'The conclusions you have drawn from your own researches on the Diaries for these two years are substantially correct. Sarah is difficult enough to follow in English, and we shall never be sure why she decided in 1658 suddenly to begin recording her confidences in indifferent French – she reverts to English of course in 1660. The fact that she was resident during these years for some of the time in Bruges but for most of it in Brussels clouds rather than clears the mystery. Servants in her households in those two cities would have been a good deal more familiar with French than with English, so it is doubtful that the change of language was intended to outwit the prying domestics.

Of the three lovers mentioned – again, circumspectly, by first names only – Fernando and Carlos were presumably Spanish. The third, Richard, deserves further investigation, having such a roundly Anglo-Saxon ring about him. We noted there was a Richard in the Diary of 1663 and deduce it may be the same man.

It is not so surprising that Sarah actually came to England and returned to the Continent during 1659. The risk of such a journey for a lady of substance in the last year of the Protectorate would have been, if not negligible, then at least calculable. Arriving and leaving through Southampton apparently without disguise or subterfuge was nevertheless daring, but quite in keeping with the lady's character.

As to her visit to Mitchell Stoke, our translations and readings have produced little more than you have gleaned already. It is clear that as the result of a letter written to her by her husband in 1644, and delivered to her in Paris two years later, Sarah knew that her jewellery and other household valuables had been hidden by him in a subterranean chapel. She retrieves the valuables, sells them in Winchester on the way back to Southampton, and hands the proceeds to the impoverished King Charles in Brussels – a credit to her acuity if not entirely to her generosity. The money involved must have been repaid a hundred times over in the course of the years following the Restoration. In any event the action finally explains the reason for the King's later benevolence to a courtesan well past her physical prime.

We are intrigued at the consummate ease with which Sarah appears to have collected *mes bjioux et mes argenteries*. The hiding place being a subterranean chapel, we assume she refers to the crypt of the parish church. Though this hardly sounds the safest of secret repositories, it would certainly make for easy access. It is not clear, however, why Sarah takes "the only passage open, not from the house". The assistance she obtains from the villagers in fetching and carrying is again a reflection on the times. No doubt they were aware that the usurping family resident in Mitchell Hall had its days there numbered.

We have no way to knowing what was contained in what we roughly translate as "the papers ruined by damp" and which Sarah discards as worthless on the return journey. If she had thought to preserve her husband's letter for our perusal no doubt we should have had a clearer idea of the nature of documents considered important enough to preserve along with the family plate.

Altogether we are jointly of the view that these Diaries add immeasurably to the value of the others you found earlier and that an edited version in one volume would, after further research, be of considerable historic interest as well as unquestionably a commercial success.'

The document ended with two signatures above the address 'Hertford College, Oxford', followed by the date.

Treasure replaced the papers in the order and position in which he had found them on the bedside table. The contents had had no immediate significance for him. Certainly they went some way to explaining Moonlight's refusal to admit the existence of the diaries referred to. Presumably he was planning some literary and historical coup, a fact which he might well have divulged within a circle of close friends, but not in the presence of Dankton who for some reason had evidently been dropped as collaborator. Nothing Treasure had read helped in any way to lighten his concern. His host was sufficiently informed to realize that the publica-

tion of some seventeenth-century diary, no matter how racy
and intimate the text, would hardly generate the funds
required to re-purchase Mitchell Hall.

Closing the dressing-room door behind him, Treasure
began walking towards his own room when he heard a
movement in the hall. A light was still burning in the porch
and it illuminated the figure of Arthur Moonlight in the act
of closing the front door. Moonlight looked up. 'Hello,
Mark, still about? – thought I'd finish off that lock in the
church,' he offered in an over-hearty tone, and as reason
for his late return. 'Like a nightcap?'

Treasure glanced at his watch. It was twelve-thirty. He
decided that the curious story of Mr Happenwack as well
as the confession he intended making to Moonlight about
reading the diary report could both wait for the morning. He
had switched off the bell on Moonlight's telephone and
considered that this underwriting of an undisturbed night
was probably the best service he could provide his friend
at this particular time.

'No, thanks, Arthur,' Treasure called down softly in order
not to wake Elizabeth.

Chief Inspector Bantree examined his watch in the wispy
moonlight that some time since had relieved the dark and
cloudy sky. 'Sergeant,' he exclaimed, 'it's nearly one o'clock.
That means we've been on this job twelve hours, and it's
not solved yet. You should be ashamed: simple little case of
suspected murder and you're standing there baffled . . .
No wonder the Chief Superintendent's not allowing us any
toys.'

Wadkin closed the gate of PC Humble's village police
house behind them. It was a neat, modern brick abode some
fifty yards along from the vicarage. The two began the walk
back to Mitchell Hall where Bantree had left his car. His
telephoned report to Headquarters had produced precisely
the response he had expected. The curious case of Horace
Worple was being afforded very low priority, at least for
the remainder of the night. The Thames Valley Police, in

all its branches, had more than enough work for its available manpower without sparing patrol cars to lie in wait at all strategic points for a fugitive Filipino.

A solitary motor-cycle patrolman was stationed at the corner opposite the church. He saluted the Chief Inspector and gave Wadkin a friendly nod.

'Well, it's all yours till four a.m. I'm afraid, Morgan,' said Bantree cheerfully. 'Keep your eyes skinned, and in the unlikely event of your sighting an Oriental approaching down the middle of the road, whistle up reinforcements fast on your radio.' Then he added more seriously, 'And I mean that: the chap's dangerous and he may be armed.'

'Very good, sir.'

The two senior men continued along the road.

'Right,' said Bantree, 'I'll drop you home on the way through Didcot.' The Inspector lived in Abingdon. 'Ring me at home from the Station around eight with an up-date on anything new they've picked up at Old Windsor. There might be something on the Filipino by then too.'

'Could be, sir, but I imagine the chap's miles away by now. The tracker dog we had here just went round in a circle, ending up at the swimming pool. His handler thinks Fred – er, that's what they call him, sir – got a lift outside the Golf Club.'

'Fred was working at the swimming pool this morning?'

'Yes, sir. According to Johnnie, their foreman, he speaks no English at all, so we ought to be able to pick up his progress when he gets hungry. We have a general alert out for him. The others should be half way to Manchester by now.'

The Inspector looked thoughtful. 'I suppose we did the right thing letting them go.' Then, as though mindful that evidence of indecision in a senior officer might be bad for morale: 'Too many unpromising suspects are much worse than too few – they get in the way. This can hardly have been a group crime, although I think more than one person must have been involved.'

'You mean Fred had an accomplice who knew the way to Old Windsor?'

The Inspector grimaced. 'Fred, the fierce Filipino who speaks no English, working closely with an ordained minister of the American Episcopal Church familiar with the location of deserted boat-houses. One of them would have to be good at sign language.' He paused, and sighed. 'There's no logic to it, is there? But my money's still on the Reverend Happenwack. He'll be tailed day and night for the remainder of his rubber-necking visit – which according to him is three days.'

'Isn't he a bit of a long shot, sir?'

'Not if you take the testimony of Mr Mark Treasure seriously. Merchant bankers – and he's a big one – are the best poker players in the business, but they don't tell lies and they don't invent stories. No, we've got a bit to learn yet about Mr Happenwack, and hopefully we should have it from the States before morning.'

As they reached the car, Bantree glanced back along the still, deserted main street of Mitchell Stoke, then at Mitchell Hall behind them, which was in darkness save for a chink of light showing between the nearly drawn curtains of a single upstairs window. The Inspector's gaze stopped there for an instant while he searched for and found a myriad reasons why law-abiding citizens permitted the normal hours of sleep should not take advantage of their good fortune. He turned back to Wadkin. 'Jump in. I'm for bed.'

The departure of the Inspector's car brought a sigh of relief from the figure clad in overalls watching the scene from one of the darkened upstairs windows of Mitchell Hall. The vigil was over at last. The business of uncovering the most momentous literary discovery since the finding of the Dead Sea Scrolls was about to begin.

CHAPTER XVII

The explosion took place at one-twenty exactly. No more shattering event had occurred in Mitchell Stoke since a night in September 1943 when a German pilot had parachuted on to the vicarage greenhouse and promptly surrendered to an aged priest clad in pyjamas and a gas mask.

Constable Humble was out of bed lacing up his boots almost before the echoes of the blast had receded. A moment later he was unlacing them again because they prevented him from putting on his trousers.

Mr and Mrs Banquet sat up in bed like two puppets jerked to life by the same string. 'It's that North Sea gas,' said Mrs Banquet with conviction. 'I knew it. I said it wasn't safe. Close the window quick.' Her husband adjusted his pullovers preparatory to obeying the instruction.

Bishop Wringle raised his head from the pillow, observed that his wife had left the room, wished that their bathroom plumbing generated a little less noise, and went back to sleep.

Timothy Trapp and Thelma Goodbody cannoned into each other on the vicarage landing. 'Are you all right, Thelma?'

'Yes, darling, are you?' Miss Goodbody was over-decorous in borrowed pyjamas so large that neither her hands nor feet were allowed to protrude. This gave her a waif-like appearance that Timothy found irresistible. He took her in his arms and kissed her.

Miss Goodbody giggled. 'Did you arrange that bang just for this?'

'Don't be ridiculous.'

'Oh, I don't mind. I was just interested. But if you didn't, don't you think we should find out what's happened?'

'Good idea. Go back and put some clothes on quickly.'

Bach positioned himself expectantly at the front door, ready to retrieve.

Mark Treasure reacted more promptly than anyone else. He was still dressed when the noise of the explosion erupted through the night. He noted the time in a reflex action, and hurried on to the landing. Elizabeth Moonlight was at the door of her room, looking dazed. 'Mark, what was it?'

'An explosion of some sort – might be a gas main, but it sounded like dynamite. Tell Arthur I'm going to investigate.' He hesitated. 'Stay in the house like a good girl till I come back.'

'Yes, sir!'

For reasons of their own – some of them related by circumstances – Moonlight, Scarbuck, and Speke-Jones were all of them fully dressed and very much alert at the time of the explosion.

Motor-cycle Patrolman Morgan was a well-trained and observant officer. Despite the leather flaps and earphones that covered his ears, he pinpointed the likely area of the explosion although he had seen no flash. It had come from the far side of the churchyard or else from just beyond the wall to the Hall. No one had entered the churchyard from his end in the hour he had been sitting in patient vigil, nor had anything else happened that could have been regarded as suspicious. If the violent and powerful eruption had been caused by human agency, then that agent's entry had most likely been effected from the Hall area, which meant, in PC Morgan's experience, that his exit would be made the same way. Being a mobile policeman, PC Morgan elected to ride along the road to the Hall instead of running through the churchyard, which enabled him at the same time to call up his radio control and report that the bombers were out in Mitchell Stoke.

'It came from the other side, Officer,' Treasure had halted beside the open gate that led from the Hall garden into the churchyard as the beam from the motor-cycle headlight swept across him. PC Morgan had caught sight of the banker's hastening figure as he had driven around the side of the Hall, and common sense had dictated that he should bear down upon, and apprehend, the only person in view two minutes after a noisy unexplained incident. He manoeuvred the motor-bike around the edge of the swimming pool, braked to a halt between Treasure and the gateway, parked the machine with the engine running, and dismounted.

'Your name, sir . . .'

'Is Treasure. I'm staying with Sir Arthur Moonlight at the Dower House. I've been helping Chief Inspector Bantree with his investigations all day, and I suggest that if you have any more questions you ask them as we go along. The explosion came from beyond this wall. Come on.'

Treasure plunged through the gateway, followed by a mildly affronted patrolman not entirely convinced that matters were proceeding in an orthodox way, but satisfied that the only character available to be suspected was jogging ahead of him literally under his surveillance.

Treasure suddenly halted and pointed ahead. 'Look, the floor of the cenotaph, it's been blown wide open.'

The only cenotaph known to PC Morgan stood in Whitehall, but his lack of familiarity with architectural terminology was no hindrance to his understanding of Treasure's exclamation. It was clear enough that the base of what looked like a small bandstand a few yards ahead had recently acquired a hole in the middle. Chunks of concrete and flagstone littered the immediate area, and the air was still heavy with dust and the reek of what the policeman recognized as explosives.

'I wouldn't stand under that roof, sir.' But Treasure ignored the admonition. He had too much faith in the structural principles employed by the designer of the cenotaph to believe that the blowing of the relatively neat, square hole he was examining in the centre of the floor would bring down the rest of the edifice if it had not done so already. Even in the circumstances, he was unable to resist a spontaneous mental tribute to the genius of the cenotaph's designer. He then applied a good deal more thought to the likely identity and the professional skill of whoever it was had arranged such unconventional access to whatever lay beneath the floor

without damaging or even apparently endangering the rest of
the unique little edifice. Before his calculations on this score
reached their inevitable conclusion – but only just – both
Treasure and Constable Morgan swung round to look in the
direction of the Hall and the source of a thunderous noise
easily identified as the merciless revving of a motor-cycle
engine.

'My bike!' cried the patrolman, racing back along the
path toward the gate. Treasure fell in behind him, offering up
a silent prayer that the stealing of a police motor-cycle was
not now to be the latest bizarre supplement to the inexplicable
behaviour pattern that day of General Sir Arthur Moonlight, late of the Royal Engineers.

Nine hours in a cold, damp tunnel had done little to assuage
the fear in the heart and mind of tiny Fred. Apart from the
unsuitable clothing he was wearing, his discomfort was
increased by the fact that he had eaten nothing since midday.
The situation would have been more bearable had he not
been aware of his close proximity to abundant supplies of
food. He was not without a certain native cunning, and he had
determined to return to the Filipino dormitory in the basement of the Hall at daybreak, relying on his older brother
Johnnie to provide whatever protection might be required
against further assault from his fat tormentor. It was possible
also that at the start of a new day the boss-man would have
found other people to persecute, since the object of his
attacks seemed to be governed more by proximity than by
provocation.

In all this, Fred had discounted the likelihood of calls
from the inner man. Quite simply, he became very hungry.
Without upsetting his major strategy, there seemed no reason
why he should not slip into the Hall through an open window,
take some food, and return to his tarpaulin-shrouded hiding
place. On arrival at the Hall, he was thwarted in this aim
by his failure to find a window open or capable of being
opened. Worse than this, peering into that lower part of the
building that had been the home of himself and his com-

patriots for nearly two weeks, he saw that it was empty – not only of people, but also of sleeping bags, trestle tables, and all the impedimenta they had brought with them. His brother and the others had gone, vanished, disappeared without word or trace. Fred began to weep, silently, but his whole small body heaved with grief. He was alone, deserted, left perhaps as the singular object for further harassment by the demon Englishman.

In a mood of deep despair Fred made his way back towards the tunnel where he could consider his plight in familiar and safe surroundings. It was during this progress that he witnessed the awful act – a scene that heaped terror upon existing misery. He saw a man struck down by another with such ferocity as to make him wish he had never left his native Mindanao where at least such things were expected and where a man comported himself accordingly – self-protected and on his guard.

It was then that Fred made his mistake. Circling the swimming pool with the same stealth he had employed throughout this nocturnal perambulation, but with the return to the haven of his hiding place uppermost in his mind, he fell over a wheelbarrow. It was because he had been watching the movements of the man who had carried out the assault that he had been careless about his own actions. Picking himself up, he quickly realized there was no further point in attempting to hide his presence. He had been heard, and now he had been seen by the man at the northern end of the swimming pool who a moment before had dispatched his first victim with a violent blow on the head into the bottom of the excavation, and with the club he was still holding in his hand.

For the second time that day, instant flight in the cause of self-preservation became Fred's only consideration. Yet before he had time even to turn away from the figure as startled at discovery as he was himself, and happily separated from him by the length of a very deep hole, a great explosion rocked the ground on which he was standing and momentarily dazed as well as deafened him.

Had Fred been of a contemplative disposition this would have been the moment for him to consider the evident absurdity of his having accepted to leave his unruly native land for the safety and rewards of working in Britain. In the course of less than one day he had been kicked in the stomach by a parson, shot by a golf-ball, narrowly escaped additional hurtful, and conceivably unnatural, bodily assault, had been forced to defend himself before being turned into a common fugitive, starved, and then deserted. Now, having witnessed a murder and qualified as the killer's next victim, he had been close enough to an explosion reasonably to assume that it had been intended for his personal destruction.

It was only a summation of these thoughts that went through Fred's mind as the surprise of the blast jerked him off balance and toppled him one step backwards to the very edge of the swimming pool. His arms flayed the air in a useless attempt to avert the inevitable. A moment later he was free-falling through ten feet to the bottom of the excavation, involuntarily preparing himself for painful impact with the ground. Fortunately, the heavy rainfall earlier had resulted in the accumulation of nearly a foot of water at the deep end of the pool. Below this the ground was exceptionally wet and muddy so that while Fred could hardly have claimed the pleasure from his dive that future users of the finished pool would enjoy, his fall was nevertheless well cushioned.

Caked in mud, very wet, but unhurt, Fred rolled himself over and grasped the edge of the tarpaulin sheet that shrouded the side of the pool, searching the while for the figure he had last seen hovering at the other end. The man was moving quickly down the long side of the pool furthest away from Fred, peering intently at the dark corner into which the Filipino had fallen. Fred calculated the man's next action, and decided his own best move was to retreat behind the tarpaulin into comparative safety. It was at this moment that simultaneously a door banged somewhere in the middle distance, lights began to appear in the upstairs windows of the Hall, and the sound of Patrolman Morgan's engine rent the still night air.

Fred remained where he was and watched the advancing figure hesitate, then cast a backward glance to the upper storey of the Hall behind him. The man looked again in Fred's direction as well as at the still form of his victim spreadeagled, face downwards, at the shallow end of the pool. The sound of the motor-cycle engine was coming closer. The man hesitated no longer. He turned and hurried into the shadow of the house as the sound of running foot-steps became audible from the direction of the Dower House.

Through an accident of fate, while Fred could boast very few accomplishments in life, he was more at home in the saddle of a motor-cycle than he was anywhere else. He and his brother had never had a home in the accepted sense, and the shanty they inhabited was more a workshop and shelter for their prized and only possession than it was a dwelling for themselves. That possession was a thirty-year-old motor-cycle that had begun life as a 150 c.c. BSA but which could now boast such an assortment of parts and patches as to make its real provenance a matter for conjecture, even by experts. Despite its decrepitude, the machine provided the brothers with a livelihood better than they could earn as fishermen, employed, as it was, as the fastest and most efficient carrier of goods, messages, and often passengers around the island on which they lived. At least, this had been the situation until a few months earlier when even the ingenuity of the two self-taught mechanics had failed to revive the outworn engine after what both had recognized as a definitely terminal splutter. The object of joining the work-gang recruited for England had been to raise the money for a new, or at least newer, machine.

Crouching in the corner of the swimming pool, three-quarters hidden by the tarpaulin, Fred had witnessed the encounter between Treasure and PC Morgan, and surrep-titiously watched them both depart in the direction of the explosion. Left behind was a vision in gleaming steel and chrome, a purring, powerful, perfect example of the ultimate

in the motor-cycle manufacturer's art. Even had Fred been
capable of rational action, then he might still have followed
his natural inclination to seize upon the sure, familiar method
of escape and salvation that presented itself. Hauling himself
up by the side of the tarpaulin, Fred was astride the machine
a few seconds after the owner had disappeared through the
gate. It did not take him much longer to familiarize himself
with the location of the essential controls. He had no idea
where he was going except that the further it was from where
he was starting, the better he would like it. He gave the
throttle a twist and listened to the reassuring burst of power
that came from beneath him. The headlight of the machine
seemed to illuminate the whole area before him so that he
could easily follow the track made in the soft ground by
Patrolman Morgan's entry.

At the main gate of Mitchell Hall Fred halted the machine.
To the left the road was flanked by buildings on both sides –
evidence of the existence of people, motor-cars and thus
agents of pursuit. To the right lay what looked like open
country and a clear road. Fred turned right – to the Golf
Club, and a dead end.

CHAPTER XVIII

George Scarbuck stood on the edge of his future swimming
pool wringing his hands in anguish. A casual observer might
well have assumed he was some lunatic preparing to dive,
fully clothed, into the shallow end of the empty hole.
Treasure and Patrolman Morgan raced into view through
the churchyard gate.

'It was Fred,' cried Scarbuck, seeing the two men. 'He's
pinched a motor-bike – I saw him – And there's a body here
in the pool. I think it's Eustace Dankton. Oh Lord!'

'Constable,' said Treasure, assuming command, 'you'd
better see to things here and I'll get after that maniac
Filipino – my car's handy. God knows how many more

people he's going to write off if someone doesn't catch him.'

Treasure began to move off in the direction of the Dower House just as Arthur Moonlight walked on to the scene. At the same time Trapp came through the gate at the double, clad in Royal Marine battledress, followed by a breathless Thelma Goodbody – in evening dress.

'Come with me, Timothy,' said Treasure, confident that he was recruiting wisely for a militant posse. He turned to Moonlight. 'Arthur, we've got another body. Get Scarbuck to ring the police.'

Constable Morgan suppressed the obvious protest that he was the police – humiliated by the disappearance of his high-powered charger and his means of instant radio communication. Coping single-handed with unexplained explosions, bodies in swimming pools, and surrounded by possible suspects, it was to his credit and relief that he accepted Treasure's orders and priorities. The banker's air of authority qualified him as the bystander best suited to render the police assistance in the circumstances, and Constable Morgan watched him disappear without misgiving.

'The car's over here,' said Treasure, pointing to the near side of the Dower House. Trapp was abreast of him, Bach was ahead enjoying the race, while Miss Goodbody was making fair progress in fourth position. 'Stop a second. Listen!' Treasure grasped Trapp's shoulder. The noise of the motor-cycle engine, which a moment before had diminished almost to the point of inaudibility, was suddenly increasing again, as though the machine was approaching rather than leaving the village.

Fred had taken the only course open to him. His flight to freedom had come to an abrupt halt half a mile along the road when he very nearly collided with a stout steel gate, securely locked and spanning the whole thoroughfare.

Some months before, the one hundred and nine affluent householders who comprised the membership of the Mid-Stoke Estate Residents' Association had corporately decided that even if they had to suffer the increasing hazard of nocturnal robbery, they could do something to diminish the quantity and weight of possessions lifted, as it were, from under their somnolent noses.

All five access roads to the golf-course had therefore been fitted with gates kept locked between the hours of midnight and six a.m. Nor was it possible to circumvent the obstacles with a machine as narrow even as a motor-cycle, a fact Fred soon discovered.

Six-foot-high, thick-wire fences with concrete stanchions had been erected around the whole perimeter of the golf-course. Fred rode scramble-style on the uneven ground beside one of these for several hundred yards. Despite the weight of the machine, by standing in the saddle the diminutive but experienced Filipino was easily able to control his course. After a few moments of fruitless searching, though more confident of his mount, Fred gave up hope of finding a gap in the fence and turned back to the road. The tarmac regained, the rider made a full-throttled advance on Mitchell Stoke.

As Treasure eased the Rolls through the stone-pillared gateway of the Dower House, Fred flashed past at sixty miles an hour.

'There he goes,' cried Miss Goodbody unnecessarily from the back seat. Treasure did not really approve her presence in the car, but there had been no time to argue the point as she had tumbled in beside Trapp. Bach had been permitted aboard for broadly the same reason.

'Hold tight, this may be an exciting ride,' said Treasure, gunning the accelerator and correcting the tail swing of the car as he centred it on the still-wet road. The rear lights of the motor-cycle were clearly in view. Fred had slowed to take the corner in the road beside the church. Although he had raked the machine ready to turn left, suddenly he braked hard, swayed to the right, then plunged straight ahead and was quickly lost to the beam of the Rolls-Royce headlights. Fred felt a good deal more at home on what looked like a dirt track than he did on a mechanized surface; he was also fairly certain that whatever was coming up behind him was too big to follow him further on the route he had chosen.

'He's taking the bridle way to the river,' said Trapp.

'Then we have to know whether he goes north or south when he gets to the towpath,' replied Treasure, bringing the big car to a halt exactly where PC Morgan had been keeping vigil earlier. From here they could watch the motor-cyclist descend the short slope to the river bank. He turned the machine left, and although it was then almost lost from sight by a line of trees, they could judge the speed and ease of its progress by the flickering side flashes from its lights. They also became aware of one of the reasons why Fred had abandoned the road.

Police Constable Humble, finally dressed for duty, was approaching from the opposite direction at a snail's pace behind the wheel of his Panda car. Since the driver's door was wide open and since Humble could hardly have been in so much of a hurry that he had not had time to shut it, obviously something was amiss. As though to confirm this point, Humble alighted from the car which, although it continued silently to make some progress down the centre of the road, was quickly left behind as its owner sprinted ahead toward the Rolls.

'Battery's flat,' announced Mitchell Stoke's resident enforcer of law and order through the window of the Rolls, his normally reedy alto approaching an anguished falsetto.

'Well, it's still moving,' said Miss Goodbody in some surprise.

'Oh, Mother's pushing at the back,' announced Humble casually and not, as it happened, quite accurately, for it was at that moment that the front wheels of the driverless little car turned down the camber of the road. Gently, but inevitably, the vehicle rolled towards an unprotected ditch. 'Put the brake on, Mother,' screamed Constable Humble.

Far from being in any position to execute this last directive – even if she had understood the mechanics involved – Mrs Humble was now revealed, standing on the crown of the road gasping for breath. Clad in a woollen dressing-gown over a flannel nightdress and bedroom slippers adorned with fluffy bobbles, she might have been an incongruous, fading apparition as she now sagged slowly to the ground. Meantime, the car she had been so gamely propelling rolled into the ditch.

'Vincent, you idiot, your mother's not well enough . . .'

Treasure cut the Vicar short. 'Thelma, nip out and get her home.' Mrs Humble had rallied at the sitting position, demonstrating that her experience had not been terminal. 'Humble, jump in the car.' Treasure judged the policeman might own a better knowledge of local by-roads than either Trapp or himself.

Miss Goodbody obeyed the order and was already at Mrs Humble's side as the Rolls swept by. 'Course I would 'ave me curlers in,' was the older woman's breathless but re-assuringly normal comment at the sight of her elegant aide.

Treasure quickly explained the situation to Constable Humble. 'How far can the chap get along that bridle path on a motor-bike?' he asked as he raced the big car along the road he knew ran roughly parallel to the river for some distance.

'Well, by rights vehicular traffic's not allowed . . .'

'Vincent, don't be a bloody fool,' cut in the Vicar. 'We're not interested in the bye-laws. Are there any obstacles on the path he can't get round with a motor-bike?'

Humble considered the question. 'Er, no . . . he can go all the way to Goring if he wants.'

'What happens then?' demanded Treasure sharply. The road was temporarily veering away from the river and there was now no way of telling whether they were keeping up with the fugitive, or even whether he was still following the bridle path.

'He'll come out in Thames Road or Cleeve Road – it all depends,' replied Humble without further qualification. Then in mitigation he added, 'They both end in T-junctions with the main road just this side of the Goring and Streatley Bridge. But there are three or four roads leading up to the road we're on from the bridle path.'

'No, he'll stick to the river,' said Treasure firmly. This was also the opinion of Royal Marine Reserve Lieutenant

Trapp, who had already credited the Filipino with the sense to take whatever tactical advantage he could from the terrain.

'So we have to beat him into Goring,' Treasure observed quietly as he saw the speedometer needle move up to ninety. They were passing through open country, rolling farmland rising to the left of them while on the right, where the ground sloped downward to the river valley, they passed small clusters of houses, and side roads posted to the villages and hamlets that punctuated the progress of the Thames. 'Keep an eye open at the junctions just in case.' Treasure himself was concentrating too hard on the twisting road ahead to follow his own injunction.

Constable Humble, in the front seat, tried surreptitiously to fasten his seat-belt and stopped worrying about his mother as the Rolls swept forward at a hundred miles an hour.

'There he is,' cried Trapp, 'I can see his headlight.'

'He's still on the bridle path, sir,' said Humble, who now had the seat-belt so tightly fastened that he could only move his arms and head. 'It leaves the river about here and moves up closer to the road.' They passed a signpost.

'Two miles to Goring,' cried Trapp.

'We're coming to a built-up area, sir,' said Humble, conscious of his responsibilities to any unsuspecting citizen who might take it into his head heedlessly to cross the road at two in the morning. Treasure braked the car as it made the sharp descent to a crossroads, but accelerated again up the hill on the other side.

A minute later Humble spoke up again. 'We need to turn right over the railway soon, sir . . . It's easy to miss the turning,' he finished apologetically, and really meaning it would be impossible to take the sharp bend to the railway bridge at sixty miles an hour. Treasure had worked this out for himself; he knew the road well enough.

'If Fred doesn't cross the river bridge, can he find the towpath to Pangbourne on this side?'

'Not without local knowledge, sir . . . I mean it would be difficult to find if you'd never been here before . . . This is the turning, sir.' Humble held on to the seat as Treasure practically stopped the car before swinging it right and on to the bridge. Bach had long since given up striking a dignified pose on the rear seat and was lying on the floor under his master's legs, wishing the journey would end.

Treasure threaded the car through the tortuous main street of Goring-on-Thames. As they rounded a right-hand bend the powerful headlights illuminated the river bridge area – and all of them could see another beam cutting across the road ahead at right angles.

'That could be him coming up Thames Road, sir.'

'That is him,' cried Treasure as the motor-cycle appeared from a side road on the right a hundred yards ahead of them.

Fred saw his pursuers at the moment they saw him. After a moment's hesitation, instead of turning right on to the bridge he drove the machine across the road and bumped it, expertly, down some wooden-edged steps on the other side, landing safely in a lane that ran parallel beside the bridge approach, and down to the water's edge.

'He's heading for the towpath,' said Trapp.

'He may have trouble finding it, sir . . . it's very confusing down there.'

The bridge and lock complex at Goring is a complicated affair. The lock is upstream of the bridge close to the Goring bank. The bridge to Streatley is in two parts because the unusually wide river span is broken by an island in the centre. Although a convenient topographical feature from the viewpoint of road communication, this island serves severely to concentrate the river flow, producing strong torrents of water accommodated by a wide half-circle of weirs and sluices. Most of these are on the upstream side of the bridge, but others – nearest the Streatley bank – are downstream.

Fred faced his machine towards the river. He was unprepared for the thunder of water that suddenly sounded to his left as he passed an old mill house, and he automatically steered away from it under the concrete supports of the bridge. Because of this, his headlight picked out the lock gate causeway which he assumed would lead to a continuous way along the river bank.

In the time that it took Fred to discover his mistake, Treasure had squeezed the Rolls through a narrow open gate and as close to the river as he could get without charging a line of steel posts. Trapp was out of the car with Humble close behind him before Treasure had brought it to a halt.

'He'll come back to the towpath on the left,' the Vicar cried over his shoulder. 'Come on, we're going to stop him.'

Humble had heard of Horatius' gallant stand, but he doubted the ability of two unarmed men to prevent someone on a 650 c.c. Triumph motor-cycle from going where he pleased. He had immediate forebodings about a nasty accident in which he was likely to be the chief or at best the joint victim. It was then that he noticed the neat pile of short oak stakes just inside the gateway of a house on the left. 'Here you are, Vicar,' he cried, as much in relief as in triumph. 'One each.'

There had been no time to lose. As Trapp and the Constable took up their armed stance at the open entrance to the river path, Fred abandoned his search for an exit from the triangle of land that ended at the lock, but he had found his bearings and worked out the direction in which he should have been heading. He retraced his way under the bridge, accelerating over the uneven turf. Then to his horror the headlight of the motor-cycle lit up the two figures guarding the narrow way, both of them wielding what looked like heavy clubs.

Two years before, Fred had found himself in a similar situation. Tracking across his native island on his own motor-cycle, he had been knocked off the machine and robbed by one man armed with a club who had suddenly appeared from behind a tree. Moreover, Fred was by nature peace-loving and even law-abiding. Even if he could break through the cordon now facing him – and experience suggested he could not – he was in enough trouble already without severely injuring what he could hardly mistake as at least one uniformed policeman.

Once again Fred altered course and spurted up the lane

he had earlier descended. He easily avoided Treasure – who was in any case unarmed – with a graceful swerve, and left that honest citizen the sole recipient of a torrent of abuse heaped down upon him by an outraged householder at an upstairs window, and concerning the criminal irresponsibility of those conducting a motor-cycle rally outside his property at two in the morning.

'Be so good as to telephone the police,' shouted Treasure with a volume and authority that silenced the man – but not Bach, who was standing beside the banker venting his distaste at being harangued from unassailable upper storeys as loudly as he was able. 'Tell them the escaped Filipino – he's a murder suspect – is crossing the river to Streatley.'

'Of course, immediately,' replied the earlier complainant, who now saw Treasure joined by PC Humble and the uniformed Trapp.

The three quickly returned to the car, with Humble still clutching his oak post. Treasure reversed the Rolls at full throttle up the narrow lane to the main road, then headed the car across the bridge.

Fred was not so far ahead of his pursuers as time might have allowed. After passing Treasure he had turned right and ridden some distance along a side road which he soon determined was a cul-de-sac leading to a church. Once more he turned about and re-emerged at the bridge approach only seconds before Treasure and his companions raced back to the car.

This time Fred did not hesitate about the direction he would take. He had traversed the first bridge span and was approaching the rise of the second before the Rolls had reached the main road. It was then that the hapless fugitive concluded that fate was not on his side. Fifty yards ahead, and just beyond the bridge's end lay a scene of disaster – and worse, obstruction – that momentarily made the prospect of further flight impossible.

Spread across the whole road were the carcass and contents of what had been a heavily overloaded truck carrying a huge cargo of timber planks destined for Oxford. Fifteen minutes before, the driver had carelessly descended the steep slope from the Reading road at a reckless speed and braked suddenly at the sight of the bridge ahead. The laws of dynamism and gravity had done the rest. That part of the road and sidewalk which had remained passable immediately after the accident were now effectively blocked by an ambulance, a police car, and sundry official personnel.

Fred slowed the motor-cycle, the better to collect his thoughts. From behind him came the roar of the Rolls-Royce breasting the first part of the bridge. Retreat was impossible. Further progress on the road was equally so. It was then that he saw the gateless entrance to the left just beyond the bridge. It promised the possibility of access to another river walk; in any event it represented his only chance of liberty.

Roaring down the slope he swerved into the entrance on to a wide gravel drive. Heading on a diagonal route for the river's edge, he quickly found himself facing imminent collision with an extremely solid hedge. He swerved left and his headlight lit up what appeared to be a solid wooden causeway. He set the machine rumbling over this with, once again, the sound of thrashing water drowning the noise of the motor-cycle engine in his ears. Too late Fred realized the causeway led not to a river path but to an unbalustraded wooden cake-walk branching left at its extremity. Too late he saw the cake-walk ended behind a complicated set of sluice rods – for he was on it riding four feet above the stone-stepped shoulders of a weir.

There was no way of turning the motor-cycle, and no pathway of retreat even if this had been possible. Already the Rolls was firmly parked hard up against the narrow entrance to the wooden causeway. Abandoning the machine, Fred gazed upon the turbulent waters beneath him. He was a strong swimmer but it was difficult to measure the depth of the water for his dive – and impossible for him to know that the whole area below the surface was solid – fashioned stone and concrete. The angle of his plunge was shallow – but so was the water. He knocked himself senseless on the bottom.

Constable Humble was also a strong swimmer – with a

number of certificates to prove it. He was close behind the Filipino as the latter took to the water – too close. Humble may have had misgivings about unseating the rider of a powerful motor-cycle approaching him at speed; he had none about his ability to overpower a diminutive, unarmed fugitive in the water. His dive was less shallow than the Filipino's and too soon to profit from the other's demonstration.

It was Trapp who fished out both the semi-conscious unfortunates by sensibly wading into the shallows where the current quickly swept them. 'Lucky there's an ambulance handy,' he remarked to Treasure as they pulled the prisoner and dazed police escort on to dry concrete.

Bach came forward balancing an oak post precariously between his teeth. He dropped it as his master's feet, looked at the water, and wagged his tail in expectation.

CHAPTER XIX

The scene at Mitchell Hall resembled nothing so much as a film set – a familiar, fictional television version of what was really happening. Only the cameras were missing. Four police cars were drawn up at untidy angles in the drive. The swimming pool area was illuminated by three large arc lamps powered by a cable that snaked its way into the basement of the Hall. Groups of policemen, some uniformed, others in plain clothes, were busily examining and measuring the ground in and around the pool. A tired-looking photographer was taking flash-lamp pictures under the direction of the thoroughly wide awake Sergeant Wadkin. Various sections of the area were being converted into roped enclosures.

The Hall itself was a blaze of lights, the front door open wide. A large crowd of villagers was grouped around the gates. Most of the viewers appeared to have arrived by car and the wide variety of conveyances humped on to the road verges in both directions bore witness to the classless and compulsive attraction of whatever it was their owners expected to see and learn. Bombings or assaults were rare events in Mitchell Stoke; in combination they were irresistible – even at two-fifteen in the morning.

Treasure halted the Rolls at the Hall gates while Trapp explained to a harassed policeman that they had business inside with Chief Inspector Bantree. While this exchange was taking place an ambulance pulled out on to the road and a Land-Rover marked 'Army Bomb Disposal Unit' drove in. The appearance of the second vehicle considerably dampened the interest of some of the onlookers who made for the safety of their cars. Once inside, they were left to contemplate the effect of falling rock on their polished conveyances, and promptly drove home. The Jaguar owners left first. Actuality was asserting itself upon the minds of those who, while used to observing death and disaster by electronic means, were totally unprepared to risk becoming part of a spectacle that others might enjoy as in-home entertainment the following day.

At the suggestion of the policeman, Treasure drove on to the Dower House where parking was easier. He and Trapp then hurried across the south front of the Hall with Bach sniffing the ground ahead. Bantree interrupted a conference he was holding with a small group of officers at the side of the huge excavation. 'Mr Treasure, Vicar, I hear you've done sterling work.' He greeted the two men smilingly.

'Is Dankton dead?' asked Treasure promptly.

'No, not yet anyway. The local doctor says he took a blow at the base of the skull. It's difficult to tell the extent of the damage without an X-ray, but opinion seems to be he'll live . . . which is just as well for your fugitive Filipino.'

'I don't believe it has anything to do with the Filipino,' said Treasure.

The Inspector raised his eyebrows. 'Now that's the most interesting observation I've heard so far . . . and I've heard a few in the last fifteen minutes. I was just going into the Hall. We have Mr Scarbuck and his guests – oh, and Sir Arthur Moonlight in the salon.' Bantree let the last name slip in a casual way but he searched Treasure's face for a reaction; there was none. 'Perhaps you and Mr Trapp would join them with me?'

'Inspector, could you leave this lot for a few minutes, I . . . I think there's something in the churchyard you ought to see.'

Bantree shrugged his shoulders and smiled. 'Sure. I've got half the Thames Valley constabulary here beating bushes to no purpose. I dare say they can cope by themselves for a while. Please lead on, sir.'

'Inspector, do you happen to know where Miss Goodbody is?' enquired Trapp.

'Yes, sir, she's in the Hall with the others – or making tea there, I think.'

'Then I'll pop over and help if you don't mind.'

'Right, sir, we'll see you later.' The Inspector and Treasure made their way towards the churchyard gate.

The top of an aluminium ladder was poking through the hole blown in the floor of the cenotaph. Lights flashed in the space below. As the two men approached the spot a head emerged through the hole, attached to broad khaki-clad shoulders. The head looked up to reveal a round, good-natured face. 'Nothing to bother you here, Inspector. Nice simple little bang, arranged by experts, though.'

'Major . . . er . . . Fendrick,' said Bantree, 'this is Mr Treasure, who was first on the scene.'

The Major extracted the rest of his stout person from the hole. 'See anyone who looked like a safe-cracker?' he enquired from Treasure with a smile. 'Whoever did this knew exactly what he wanted to achieve – it's almost as if he'd done it with a cold chisel, except it would have taken longer – about a year longer. Just look at the thickness of that floor.'

'Oh, we know who did it,' said the Inspector, a statement that obviously came as a surprise both to the Major and to Treasure. 'We just needed you chaps to confirm he wasn't planning to do any more . . . Actually, you were on your way before we obtained the . . . er . . . confession.' He glanced at

Treasure who was experiencing what could accurately be described as a sinking feeling.

'Well, was it an expert?' asked Fendrick.

'If you'd call a retired Major-General in the Royal Engineers an expert, then I suppose it was,' said Bantree. Treasure's spirits sank almost without trace.

'Blimey,' commented the Major, 'has the old boy gone off his chump?'

'Not exactly. Not at all, as a matter of fact. I'm not even sure yet we can charge him with anything – except disturbing the peace.'

'Well, that's up to you, Inspector. There are no more explosives lying around, so if it's all the same to you we're off to beddy-byes.'

Treasure recovered himself sufficiently to press forward with what he was certain were revelations now more important than they had been before the Inspector's disarming announcement. 'Major,' he asked, 'can you tell me what's down there?'

'Well, apart from my sergeant, there's a chamber the size of this floor with a ceiling height of about seven feet. There's what looks like a small marble altar table on what I suppose would be the – ' he glanced at the church to get his bearings – 'yes, the east side, and there's a blocked opening on the same wall. Opposite there's a tunnel leading towards the church. My sergeant's having a wander through it now. That's the way the fuse was laid. When he surfaces we'll be able to tell you how long before the bang the fuse was lit – but I suppose you know that too?' The Inspector shook his head. 'Well, anyway, it'll all be in my report.' He turned back to the hole from which he had earlier emerged. 'Sergeant!' he bellowed into the chamber below. 'You gone to sleep down there?'

'No, Major Fendrick,' said a voice behind them, 'I decided on the round trip.' The tall bespectacled Sergeant who had appeared from the direction of the church stood beaming at the group. 'The tunnel ends in some stone steps leading up to a flagstone trap door in the crypt – elaborate chain and weight mechanism on the tunnel side, beautiful job in iron – but you wouldn't guess it was there from the crypt side in a hundred years. You spring it by turning the base of one of the legs on a stone altar. The whole thing's been oiled recently, but the works are in fair nick anyway – no rust to speak of. Incidentally, the fuse was laid from the foot of the stone steps, snaked all over the place – could have been going for up to an hour I'd say. D'you want it measured?'

The Major glanced questioningly at Bantree. 'Not necessary, Major Fendrick. My chaps can do that,' said the Inspector.

Treasure cut in. 'The aperture on the east wall, Major – what's it blocked with?'

The Major looked at the Sergeant who replied, 'A sort of wooden door, sir, but too long for the opening. It looks as though the top is resting on a ledge above the aperture on the far side; the bottom is three or four feet beyond – like a ramp the wrong way round.'

'D'you have a saw with you, Major?' was Treasure's next unlikely enquiry.

'Oh, we're better equipped than Selfridge's,' beamed Fendrick. 'Sergeant, show the gentleman your battery-operated cutter and all forty-seven handy attachments – slices smoked salmon a treat.'

The Sergeant selected some equipment from a roll pack spread along the ground at his feet. 'You want me to saw through that door, sir?' he enquired with enthusiasm.

'If nobody else minds,' replied Treasure, eyeing Bantree.

The Inspector nodded approval. 'We'll come down with you, Sergeant,' he said, making for the ladder.

'Well, if it's all the same to you I'll hang on here for a gasper,' commented the Major. 'Had enough excitement for one night; it's all go in this business. Try not to be too long, I've got a chance to go parachuting at ten.'

The wooden ramp was thick but rotting. Its centre began to buckle ominously by the time the Sergeant was half way across its width with the extremely efficient saw. 'My guess is it'll cave in shortly, bringing a load of rock down with it,' said Treasure. Almost as he spoke there was a loud rending noise; the single panel of wood split onwards from the saw cut, and collapsed.

The three men moved back quickly to the tunnel on the far side of the little chamber as a small load of rock rubble tumbled through the aperture. But the tumult was quickly over. The angled door had disintegrated more through its own weakening than through the comparatively light weight of stone resting on its further side.

'You all right down there?' cried Fendrick, fanning away the cloud of dust that rose through the hole to the open air.

'Fine, thanks,' Bantree called back, already intrigued at the sight illuminated by the beam of the torch he was carrying and beyond the small pile of rocks strewn around the opening in the eastern wall of the chamber. 'You and the Sergeant can push off now if you like. Thanks very much for your help.'

'What about the ladder?'

'We shan't be needing it,' said Treasure with assurance.

'Take it with you, Major,' called Bantree. Then, as an afterthought, he added, 'But you might tell the uniformed police sergeant at the pool where we are.'

'We may get there before him,' said Treasure.

'Yes, but it's nice to know you're not forgotten.' The Inspector stepped carefully over the rubble with Treasure close behind him.

The gallery the two men entered had evidently and originally been stone lined from floor to round-arched ceiling. It was possible to judge the original proportions – approximately five feet wide and of equal height – from the part sections in sight. It was just as evident, however, that damp and decay had gone some way to destroy the ancient corridor. A clear walk-way had been breached with modern implements. Metal stanchions and supports were reflected in the torch beam at irregular intervals. Treasure marvelled that the whole corridor had not caved in long since, and guessed that it would certainly have done so through the tremor of that night's explosion had it not been for the up-to-date strengthening.

Once inside, Treasure asked the Inspector to shine his torch back the way they had come and on to the roof area. This revealed a seven- or eight-foot-long shallow recess in the ceiling, flanked at its extremities from the chamber door by iron chains looped through ring-bolts set into the walls on either side.

'Mitchell Stoke version of a portcullis,' commented Treasure. The Inspector waited for more enlightenment. 'If you were being pursued through the gallery, a tug on those chains would bring the roof down – or rather, that wood panel we sawed through, plus the load of stones stored behind it in the roof. Very effective I should think – one of the sweeter uses of adversity.' Inspector Bantree missed the allusion.

'But who was being chased?' he asked.

'Oh, a recusant priest escaping Puritan retribution perhaps. That chamber under the cenotaph was obviously used as a chapel – probably built for the purpose.' Treasure thought for a moment. 'Yes, the dates fit perfectly. Lots of rich Catholics began making arrangements for very private worship in 1629 – rather like Americans building fall-out shelters in the 'sixties. The Moonlights may well have needed that chapel after the passing of the Solemn League and Covenant . . . That was early in 1644.'

Bantree was a Methodist but supported the ecumenical movement. He made no comment except a sigh that summed up his view on the attitudes of graceless zealots.

'Of course,' Treasure continued, 'actual pursuit may not have been the reason for blocking the gallery; concealment is another possibility.'

'You mean a search party coming along here, seeing a roof-high load of broken stone, might think they were at the end of the line?'

'Exactly – and there is another way out of the chamber beyond, of course. D'you feel a draught?'

For the first time Bantree became conscious that the air they were breathing was peculiarly fresh for an underground tunnel. He was also momentarily taken aback because Treasure had disappeared.

'Come up here, Inspector.' The disembodied voice emanated from somewhere forward and to the right of where the policeman was standing. He moved on, passing a thick stone buttress that jutted into the gallery. Immediately behind this in a recess was a short flight of stone steps set at right angles to the gallery. He mounted these to join Treasure. The two men stood shoulder to shoulder in a squat stone enclosure, rectangular in shape, with iron lattice-work set under the roof on all four sides.

'Early example of a ventilation shaft, decently disguised as a tomb. Lend me that torch a minute and watch.' With a hefty pull Treasure dislodged one of the iron grilles, at the same time he rested the torch against his chest so that the beam shone up around his face. 'Boo!' he shouted at the top of his voice.

'Very droll, Mr Treasure,' came the comment of Major Fendrick from somewhere outside, 'but don't make a habit of it. I live a somewhat sheltered life; that's enough to give a chap heart failure.' The Sergeant chuckled. The two soldiers were clearly visible packing up their gear next to the Acropolis.

'Which clears up one mystery,' said Treasure as he and Bantree stepped down into the gallery.

'Which one?' Bantree had so many on his hands.

'Last Tuesday an aged lady called Maggie Edwards dropped dead of a heart attack just where the Major was standing. I believe she was frightened by a face – probably Filipino – peering at her through that gap.'

This was the first time Bantree had heard that there might be some mystery surrounding the death of Maggie Edwards. Whether or not there was substance in Treasure's assertion, the Inspector was bound to agree that the sight of an Oriental apparently in the process of resurrection might well have an unnerving effect on old ladies. Ruefully he contemplated the need for yet another exhumation.

'There are two of those tomb-ventilators serving the

gallery,' said Treasure, pointing to the second as he and the Inspector made their way further along the tunnel. 'Quite clever, really. The gallery itself, I believe, was ready made – it must be part of the cellar of the old monastery. These interior buttresses may have been put in when the building on top was dismantled and the site covered over with earth from the excavations for the new Hall.'

Treasure was conscious that his antiquarian revelations were proving less than compulsive to a police Inspector engaged in unravelling a complicated series of crimes. Happily, the torch beam illuminating the way ahead was now shining upon a scene which in Treasure's view was about to make the whole underground excursion especially relevant to the policeman's enquiries.

A complicated tangle of tubular steel props extending from floor to ceiling appeared almost to be blocking further progress through the gallery. In fact, as the two men came up to the scaffolding it was apparent that the gallery itself was punctuated at this point by semi-circular spaces on either side, giving the whole area a width of perhaps twelve feet. The props were shoring up boards that here entirely replaced the stone vaulting of the roof itself – a good five feet higher than in the rest of the gallery. In the centre of the space beneath were what remained of the stone surrounds of a circular hole some five feet across and filled, almost to the brim, with jagged rocks covered by a thin powdering of earth.

The area was littered with discarded scaffolding equipment, steel joints and tubes, and pieces of sawn-off wooden planks. The impression of disorder thus created was more than re-flected in the arrangement of the scaffolding itself, which even to the untutored eye looked wholly unprofessional, relying more on the quantity of supports involved than on their technical arrangement.

The Inspector swung his torch beam around the nearest gallery alcove. Conspicuous amongst the rubble stood a stubby machine on two wheels. Stout hand-grips were fixed behind a square engine casing; in front protruded two steel shafts about three feet long, each bearing four narrow, burrowing-blades.

'Well, it's not exactly a lawn-spiker,' said Bantree quietly, 'but here we have Crown Exhibit Number One.' He moved over to the machine and began examining it closely but without touching any part.

'If you could throw some light on the roof again, Inspector, I think you'll find we're under the grave that Worple was digging this morning.' Treasure paused while Bantree directed the beam upwards. 'Would you accept that Worple launched himself head-first through the bottom with a lunge from his pick, broke his neck on that pile of rocks, and then somehow got caught up on the business end of that machine?'

'Hole in one, Mr Treasure – or two perhaps,' agreed the Inspector ruefully. 'And you figure that afterwards the grave was made good from below? – in a hurry by the look of it, and not by experts either.'

'Exactly: the job was complicated because of this well, or vat, or whatever it is directly underneath – hence the haphazard scaffolding.' Treasure peered about the badly lit scene. 'The chaps who erected this tangle were unskilled labourers engaged to dig a swimming pool, plus, of course, the service tunnels for the plumbing. No doubt that's what they thought this gallery was for. What they lacked in expertise they made up in ignorance – and innocence.'

'Not after they had a dead body on their hands,' commented Bantree firmly.

'Chances are the Filipinos never saw the body.'

'Could be,' said Bantree, thinking back over the reported disposition of the permanent and temporary residents of Mitchell Stoke at ten-thirty on the previous day.

'Worple kills himself; somebody gets rid of the body – I think I know how – the work force is brought in to make the grave good again from this side . . .'

The Inspector interrupted, 'And it wouldn't have taken five minutes for someone to nip up to the churchyard, chuck a foot or so of earth on the bottom of the grave, and stamp it in. That's why my people found nothing unusual when they removed the coffin.'

'So the whole affair could have been a covered-up accident – possibly the accident Happenwack . . . er . . . mentioned to me?' Treasure tried to keep any note of triumph out of his voice.

The Inspector chuckled, then shone the torch beam on his watch. He had made more progress in the previous ten minutes than he had had all day. There was time and justification for an overdue revelation of his own. 'Mr Treasure, I owe you an apology of sorts. I never doubted your statement about our American friend, but you'll appreciate his story placed me in an awkward position. If it's any consolation, Happenwack, as he calls himself, was arrested half an hour ago on the strength of information supplied by the New York State police . . .'

'On what charge?'

'Oh, illegal entry will keep him safely at Reading Police Station until morning, sir. I suspect there may be more serious charges pending. Now, I suppose you know the way out of this labyrinth?'

'Come this way, Inspector.' Treasure was considerably lighter in heart as he and the policeman picked their way through the next part of the gallery on steeply rising ground.

'Take care here, sir – it's another of your portcullises, but definitely twentieth-century by the look of it.'

The Inspector, who was now ahead of Treasure, indicated a steel-framed raft of wire mesh above their heads; it appeared to be bearing a load of earth and rubble. The raft itself was held in place at the near end – a foot or so in from the corners – by two fully extended, heavy-duty jacks. The further end, which the two men, already stooping, passed more gingerly, was held up by a pair of wooden props. Ropes attached to the bases of these hardly adequate supports threaded forwards and upwards to a double marine-block and ring-bolt in the roof.

Bantree indicated the rope end hanging loose. 'One good pull on those and out come the front supports, and down comes passable evidence of a cave-in. I see there's a spade and a pile of earth here for filling in any imperfections. Looks as though this tunnel's due for imminent closure.'

'Yes,' agreed Treasure, 'and we're now entering what might be termed the valid plumbing area.' He pointed ahead. 'Yonder lies the pool, and if I'm not mistaken this tunnel off to the left is where you lay the pipe for water inlets, or alternatively how you transport unwanted bodies under cover. Want to look?'

Bantree was already striding up the narrow side tunnel. A minute later the two men ascended to ground level in the centre of what was unmistakably a gentlemen's public lavatory in process of drastic alteration.

'The intended boiler house, I assume,' said Treasure, surveying what was left of the most expensive amenity provided by Arthur Moonlight for the tourist invasion that never happened.

The Inspector was especially interested in a six-foot gap in the entrance wall which faced directly on to the drive of Mitchell Hall. 'You could get a Volkswagen through there easily,' he continued thoughtfully. He shone the torch beam on to another wall, steadying it on a piece of gleaming porcelain. 'Hm, Twyford's I see. Well, let's hope they're still connected,' he added, advancing with alacrity.

CHAPTER XX

Arthur Moonlight sat relaxed and composed in the ante-room on the ground floor of Mitchell Hall. Throughout the questioning from Inspector Bantree he had been answering with directness and assurance. Certainly he admitted responsibility for the explosion. The cenotaph was his own property and if he chose to blow a hole in it, that was his business. He was in legal possession of the explosives used. True, they had been supplied for disposing of tree roots in the garden of the Dower House, but he was quite prepared to defend their employment for other peaceful uses. He was a qualified expert on explosives and the limits of the demolition he had arranged earlier that night were exactly those he had predicted in a letter to the Chief Constable, posted the previous afternoon. The event had caused injury to no one; he apologized for disturbing the peace and was quite ready to pay a fine for his indiscretion in this connection.

If Inspector Bantree had not been putting the questions himself, then – like Treasure and Wadkin who were also present – he might have been drawn to the conclusion that the whole smooth exchange had been rehearsed.

For his part, Treasure was delighted to see the old, commanding Arthur Moonlight replace the spiritless personality of the day before. Whatever Moonlight's motives for his bizarre action, their fulfilment had evidently lifted the great cloud of despondency his friend had been living with since Treasure's arrival.

'And of course you're prepared to give the reason for your conduct, Sir Arthur?' Bantree's question sounded almost rhetorical.

'Naturally, Inspector. I propose building a supporting column to the roof of the cenotaph. The whole structure needs strengthening.'

Sergeant Wadkin, who stood in some awe of titled persons, was the only one of the four who gave any credence to this patently absurd reply.

'Hm, well, if it didn't need it before I suppose it needs it now,' observed Bantree with a smile. Then without changing his expression he continued, 'There is, of course, the coincidence of the attack on Mr Dankton . . .'

'Which occurred long after I had set the fuse and returned to my home – at least according to the doctor who examined Dankton.'

'I can witness that, Inspector,' volunteered Treasure.

Bantree directed an amiable glance at the banker. 'To be precise, Mr Treasure, you saw Sir Arthur come in at twelve-thirty. Lady Moonlight affirms that he retired to his dressing-room shortly after one o'clock. There are no witnesses as to his whereabouts between that time and one-twenty . . .'

'Nor to mine, for that matter,' Treasure interrupted loyally.

The Inspector inwardly hoped that Treasure would not emphasize the irregularity of his presence with any more subjective offerings. The policeman had agreed to his remaining in the ante-room instead of joining those awaiting their turn for interview in the salon, partly in return for the banker's help earlier, partly to make up for the Happenwack episode, but mostly because Treasure had confidently asserted that, given some more facts to confirm a slanderous and thus unutterable theory, he believed he could provide an explanation for the night's events.

Certainly the policeman had every reason for trusting Treasure's judgement and acuity. He was satisfied already that the banker's philosophical deduction about the irrelevance of Fred the Filipino was probably correct. Treasure had observed that the little foreigner's evident abhorrence of violence made him a most unlikely suspect as Dankton's – or anybody else's – assailant. He had recounted how Fred had baulked at charging the largely defenceless Trapp and PC Humble on the towpath, and how he had considerately eschewed the opportunity to eliminate Treasure himself a moment later.

Neither Treasure nor Bantree could know that in terms of an earlier experience their explanation of Fred's conduct was not to the letter accurate, but it certainly accorded with the spirit. If the Vicar and the policeman had not been wielding wooden clubs, then Fred, with a moment more for consideration, would still have found a way of riding safely around instead of inhumanely at them.

Treasure's inspired explanation of how Worple had met his death was circumstantially promising enough to make Bantree confident that, given half an hour with the impostor Happenwack, one part of a complicated case could be closed with the certainty of a conviction. Quite how Happenwack fitted into the rest of the affair was still unclear. The brazen confidence of the man demonstrated in general by his presence in the country and in particular through his two confrontations with Treasure evoked a degree of grudging admiration from the Inspector.

Happenwack's real name was Leslie March, and in deference to the cloth and living character he had assumed, Bantree was disciplining himself to think of the man by his real name. March was – predictably in the circumstances – an actor, and first cousin to the real Reverend Happenwack, to whom he reportedly bore a close physical resemblance. In the previous year March had obtained a work permit to perform in Britain for six months. Most of this time he had spent treading the boards in minor parts at the Oxford Playhouse, but he had also appeared at theatres in Guildford, Leatherhead and Windsor. His address in England throughout the period had been a cottage in Woodstock where he had lodged with the owner – a certain Eustace Dankton.

Shortly after his return to the USA, March had been arrested and convicted on drug charges. He would unquestionably have been sent to jail had it not been for the intervention of his cousin, who had not only gone surety for his good conduct but also taken responsibility for his erring relation's rehabilitation. March had been living with his cousin ever since. Two weeks earlier he had left the clergy house at Roundtop to begin rehearsals for a play with a repertory company in Boston – or so he had told his unsuspecting cousin. In fact, March had left the country using Happenwack's identity and his passport – a document seldom required and not missed until the New York State Police had demanded to see it a few hours earlier.

All this information had been awaiting Bantree and Wadkin when they had arrived at Didcot Police Station. Following the arrest of March by the Reading Police, a search of his belongings had disclosed not only two passports – his cousin's and his own – but also a ticket for the TWA flight to Boston the next day reserved in his own name. One suitcase fully packed with personal belongings and another lightly filled with cotton wool were colouring the nature of the further enquiries in progress at Reading.

The mild admonition that Bantree decided to direct at Treasure for interrupting the questioning was, in the event, never delivered. Suddenly the door to the ante-room was thrown open, and an obviously angry Scarbuck entered, brushing aside the prohibition of a uniformed policeman who was now standing behind him looking appealingly toward his superior officer.

'All right, Constable, close the door, will you,' said Bantree. 'Now, Mr Scarbuck, I'm afraid we're not quite ready . . .'

'Well, I'm not ready either to be shut up like a flaming prisoner in my own lounge . . . my salon,' the red-faced Scarbuck corrected himself, 'while you entertain this desiccator and murderer – ' he indicated Moonlight – 'and his toffee-nosed friend. He's destroyed half the churchyard, as good as done in poor old Dankton, and as like as not made off with millions of pounds' worth of my property – or else blown it to smithereens. And all you can do is sit here chatting with him. Put him behind bars! I've half a mind to ring the 'Ome Secretary.'

'I wouldn't do that, Scarbuck, at least not until you've heard the charges against you,' said Treasure quietly.

Scarbuck swung round to face the banker. 'Charges? What charges? I've done nothing.'

Bantree decided that this irregular exchange was promising enough to warrant extension. He remained silent.

'Well, the Inspector will have to provide the right terminology, but as I see it you're guilty of criminal conspiracy with Dankton and others in failing to report a fatal accident, disposing of a dead body, and attempting to appropriate hidden valuables to which you have no title. It's also possible you could be accused of attempting to murder your fellow conspirator. No, I wouldn't ring the Home Secretary if I were you.'

'Has he gone mad, Inspector? I'll have him up for criminal libel – and you'll be my witness.'

'Slander, I think,' said Treasure coolly.

It had already occurred to the Inspector that Scarbuck might have a case. 'All in due course, sir. The Sergeant here is making notes. Meantime, since you're here, perhaps you could answer some questions. You mentioned millions of pounds' worth of your property. Could you describe the property for me, sir?'

Scarbuck dropped into a convenient armchair and sighed. 'Well, I suppose it will all have to come out now – but I'm guilty of nothing criminal. There was treasure in that tomb thing, jewels, gold plate, and more important a Shakespearean heliograph . . .'

'Holograph,' Moonlight corrected.

'There you are – ' Scarbuck stabbed a finger in the speaker's direction – 'he knows. Ask him how he knows. He's the conspirator – in league with Dankton, no doubt. If that swine was double-crossing me he deserved all he got – but it wasn't me who hit him,' he added quickly.

'How did you learn about the treasure in the tomb, sir?'

Scarbuck gave another sigh of resignation. 'Through Dankton. He found a letter, along with those diaries he pulled out of a wall somewhere. The letter was to one of this maniac's female ancestors – ' he nodded at Moonlight – 'only it was never delivered. The woman – Sarah Moonlight – had left the country before it was written, or so Dankton found out from some other diaries Moonlight was daft enough to lend him. So the treasure was still there – Dankton was sure of it.' He hesitated, then continued in more subdued tones. 'Dankton came to me with a proposition. He said whoever owned this house would automatically own the manuscript and the other things. He knew the place was up for sale but he couldn't raise the wind for the purchase price himself. He said if I bought it he'd settle for the jewels and plate plus twenty-five per cent of what the manuscript fetched. It was only later we were advised by . . . well, we were advised that the tomb didn't go with the Hall . . .'

'It certainly didn't,' put in Moonlight firmly.

'Well, that's as maybe, but legally it's what's known as

a mute point,' continued Scarbuck, establishing that he had a greater familiarity with the law than with the English language. 'And if you've got that helio – that manuscript, Moonlight, I'll fight you for it through every court in the land.' He paused. 'Well, to avoid legal . . . er . . . mis-understanding, we decided to bring the stuff out of the tomb and into the Hall – and I own the Hall, so what's found in it's mine.'

Treasure decided that less time would be wasted if Scarbuck was made aware he had been on a wild goose chase. 'The manuscript and the other valuables were removed from the cenotaph in 1659, Scarbuck, so I'm afraid you were several hundreds of years too late in your search.'

'That's your opinion – and a very convenient story if you two have the stuff tucked away somewhere.'

'Scarbuck, there's documentary proof of what I have just told you in the diary of Sarah Moonlight for the year in question.' Treasure avoided Moonlight's surprised glance.

'Mr Scarbuck – ' this was Bantree – 'as I understand it, you have just admitted responsibility for the tunnelling from the swimming pool to the cenotaph. Mr Worple fell to his death into that tunnel this morning . . .'

'I know, Inspector, but it was an accident – pure accident. I'd intended telling you about it in the morning,' Scarbuck lied, desperation quickly replacing the tone of outrage in his voice. 'I was not made aware of the facts until well after it all happened – and I was not party to the removal of the body. That was entirely Dankton's doing, bloody fool. I told him to make a clean breast of the whole affair to you – that's why I delayed telling you myself.' He ended with a hopeful look at the Inspector.

'And the lacerations on the man's chest – they were part of the accident?'

'They were, Inspector. Poor chap bounced off some stones and fell on to a tunnel borer – it wasn't going at the time, but the blades are very sharp and they must have gone round on the impact – or so Dankton told me.'

'But the grave was made good to prevent discovery of

the tunnel, Mr Scarbuck.'

'All without my knowledge, Inspector. Dankton is to blame for the whole thing . . . I hate having to disclose the facts in this way.' Scarbuck shook his head sadly to emphasize the true depths of the discomfort he was suffering.

'Quite so, Mr Scarbuck, but I have to warn you there'll be further questions on the matter. Any help you can give us on other events tonight will, I expect, be taken into account.' The implications of this remark were obvious.

'I shall give you every possible assistance in bringing the guilty to book, Inspector,' Scarbuck replied sanctimoniously, and with a side glance to ensure that Wadkin was still keeping the record.

Scarbuck then confirmed that the tunnel had been cleared ready for Dankton to enter the cenotaph chapel after removing the light rubble remaining at the door. Having transported the valuables to a place of safety, he was to bring down the roof-shaft at the swimming pool end of the tunnel to give the appearance that the gallery had not been breached beyond that point. He conveniently forgot to mention the obviously intended abandonment of the expensive but incriminating piece of boring equipment inside the blocked tunnel.

'At what time did you order Dankton to do all this, Mr Scarbuck?' Bantree put some emphasis on the word 'order'.

'That was entirely up to him, Inspector. You must understand that I was at arm's length from the whole operation. He did mention to me he'd wait until everyone had gone to bed.'

'Until the coast was clear?'

'You could say that, yes.'

'He expected no difficulty with his task – I mean it was well within the capability of one man to handle the job?'

'Oh, it would have been child's play. The Filipinos had done all the heavy work. Of course, they knew nothing about what was at the end of the tunnel.'

'No, you were the only one who had that information and a knowledge of Dankton's intentions tonight. Mr Scarbuck,

Dankton was to get all the jewels and plate, a quarter of the proceeds from the sale of a very valuable manuscript, and we have reason to believe that he and his partner were pressing you for a larger share. Since the remainder of the work was, as you describe it, child's play, wouldn't you have been better off with Dankton out of the . . . er . . . out of the picture?'

Scarbuck reared in his chair. 'This is a damned conspiracy!' He glanced around at the others. 'Here I am giving you every co-operation, and you've as good as accused me of trying to murder Dankton. What about him?' He pointed to Moonlight. 'What about the Filipino?' he roared, rising from the chair. 'What about Dankton's accomplice? You'll not get another word out of me until I've got a lawyer present.'

'Scarbuck, sit down.' Treasure spoke firmly but quietly. The other hesitated before obeying but he eventually accepted the order. 'I don't like you, and I don't like what you've been up to,' Treasure continued. 'Nevertheless, I don't believe you're a murderer and I do know you've been duped. If you think you're going to get out of all this without a penalty you're a bigger fool than I take you for. Don't make matters worse by walking away now suspected of something you haven't done. Where were you at the time of the explosion?'

'In my bedroom – I swear to God I was.' Scarbuck's tone registered he was ready to accept Treasure's intervention. Bantree sensed this and waited for the banker to continue.

'You ought to know that Arthur Moonlight has witnesses to prove he was in the Dower House at the relevant time.' Inspector Bantree let this statement pass. Treasure continued: 'The Inspector has eliminated the Filipino from his list of suspects, and Dankton's partner was under police observation miles away when the attack took place. On your own admission you were the only person who knew about Dankton's intended movements . . . or were you? Think hard, Scarbuck – this is important.'

Scarbuck looked as though he was about to burst. 'I

wasn't', he cried, 'I wasn't the only one. Speke-Jones knew·
I told him after dinner tonight that Dankton was ready to – '

The telephone on a table beside Wadkin broke in upon
whatever further revelation Scarbuck had in store. 'Reading
General Hospital, sir.' Wadkin handed the instrument to
Bantree.

'A moment, Mr Scarbuck,' said the Inspector.

CHAPTER XXI

It was half an hour since Scarbuck and Speke-Jones had
been arrested and taken into detention.

Elizabeth Moonlight was presiding over a tea party in
the study of the Dower House. Although it was twelve
hours before the normal time for such a ceremony – with
the hostess incongruously clad in a nightgown and lace
negligee – all the participants were quite unconscious of
time or appearances. To a man and woman they were hanging
on the words of Mark Treasure, who was standing before
the fireplace.

'Of course, it was downright immoral of me to have read
the report on the Diaries,' he said, 'and I apologize, Arthur,
for having done so.' Moonlight shrugged his shoulders.
'But, after that, previous and subsequent events fell into
place quite logically. Clearly, Scarbuck had come upon the
James Moonlight letter or a copy of it, almost certainly
through the agency of Dankton. The expectancy of vast
riches accounted for Scarbuck's having paid such a huge
sum for Mitchell Hall practically sight unseen. The elaborate
burrowing under the churchyard was certainly the most
circumspect way of bringing the valuables into Scarbuck
territory – he couldn't know there was another, and incidentally, far shorter and better preserved way into the chamber under the Acropolis.'

'But why didn't he just raid the monument on some dark
night and make off with the booty?' asked Trapp, who was

sitting beside Miss Goodbody on a sofa. 'That way he needn't have bought the Hall in the first place.'

'Ah, on that point he was well advised, certainly by Dankton and possibly by Speke-Jones,' Treasure explained. 'Think what was at stake. The jewellery was possibly identifiable – from pictures of the period.' Trapp stole a glance at Thelma Goodbody, who smirked. 'But more important, anyone announcing he has a Shakespearean holograph in his possession had better be in a position to explain how he came upon it, and that he's the rightful owner. For all Scarbuck knew, the thing could have been dedicated to Francis Moonlight or peppered with stage directions naming Mitchell Hall. No, if for an outlay of two hundred thousand pounds Scarbuck could prove that the manuscript was "discovered" on his property – and he was arranging to do just that – he was home and dry. No doubt Dankton was briefed to pull the thing out of a wall somewhere in Mitchell Hall – or possibly from the side of the swimming pool. And remember, Scarbuck had gone to special pains to establish in the sale deed that he was the rightful owner of the Hall and everything in it – and in his view that meant a great deal more than the fixtures and fittings.' Treasure looked across at Moonlight. 'There's the other consideration, of course, that you can't get into the Acropolis from above without literally blowing it up and bringing the whole village out to see what you're doing.'

'A Shakespeare holograph,' said Miss Goodbody to nobody in particular, but with reverence and awe.

'Worth a packet, I should think,' observed the practical Trapp.

'Oh Timothy, it's not what it would be worth, it's what it would prove,' the girl admonished. 'Don't you see, it could have shown once and for all that Shakespeare existed – all the myths and libels about Bacon and the rest could have been exploded. I'll bet the play was *As You Like It*.'

'Well, whatever it was, Sarah Moonlight chucked it out of the carriage window on the way to Winchester,' said Moonlight abruptly. 'Thelma's right about the importance

of the thing, but it was the money Scarbuck was after. I
think three million was a bit hopeful even so. Parliament
would never have allowed such a thing out of the country,
so it wouldn't have gone to America for a fancy price.
Probably it would have been bought for the British Museum
at a reasonable price after a "ring" on the bidding. British
dealers are pretty sensible about such things.'

'But I still don't understand where Mr Speke-Jones
comes in – and why he tried to murder poor Mr Dankton.'
This was Elizabeth.

'Attacking Dankton was entirely in character,' explained
Treasure. 'Speke-Jones is an opportunist *par excellence*. I
doubt he's ever done anything quite so criminal before,
and he could have saved himself the trouble if he'd waited
until Dankton had come out of the tunnel empty-handed.
I think he was as convinced as the others that the holograph
existed, but he simply couldn't afford to have it revealed for
some days – ideally weeks. My guess is that he knew Dankton
had to close the tunnel, with that raft of rubble I told you
about, after he'd emptied the chapel. That could well have
been a noisy procedure that might have attracted someone's
attention – remember, Speke-Jones knew there were police
about the place – we all did. So he decided to hang about by
the pool and then reason with Dankton when he turned up.'

'But why didn't he just get hold of Dankton before he left
the Hall?' asked Trapp.

'Oh, that's easy enough to figure,' Treasure answered
confidently. 'Speke-Jones had to persuade the chap to post-
pone the plan he'd agreed with Scarbuck, either through
bribery or perhaps even blackmail. I doubt he'd considered
violence until it came to the point. In any circumstance,
though, he needed Dankton well clear of further contact with
Scarbuck.'

'And if he had killed Mr Dankton for refusing to co-
operate, then Scarbuck might have been the prime suspect,'
put in Thelma Goodbody.

'With no witnesses, and nothing to connect Speke-Jones
with Dankton, you're quite right,' said Treasure, 'and that's

something Speke-Jones may well have taken into account when he decided to clobber Dankton. I don't know what his plan was after that – perhaps he didn't either. If he knew about the arrangements in the tunnel, he might have decided to drag Dankton in there, then make it look as though he'd been killed by a roof-fall. It was little Fred who cooked his goose, of course. When he came to in Reading Hospital, Fred started babbling about seeing Dankton, whom of course he knew, and Speke-Jones, whom he remembered from the golf course, talking together at the pool before Speke-Jones biffed Dankton with a wooden pole. The amazing thing was that the person nearest his bed understood every word he said. She was a nursing auxiliary from the same part of the Philippines as Fred. She translated the whole thing to the policeman watching over Fred. Of course, Speke-Jones denied everything until Inspector Bantree told him that Dankton had recovered consciousness at the Radcliffe in Oxford . . .'

'Has he?' exclaimed Elizabeth. 'Oh, I'm so glad.'

'As a matter of fact he hasn't,' said Treasure, 'but Bantree knew there was a sporting chance of his doing so by tomorrow so he took a chance to get a confession. Once Speke-Jones realized he couldn't be accused of anything more serious than assault, he coughed up.'

'I'm not sure that was entirely cricket,' remarked Thelma Goodbody primly.

'Neither is attempted murder,' observed the Vicar. 'But tell us why Speke-Jones needed to keep the discovery of the holograph quiet – you said for some weeks.'

'Well, that's privileged information,' replied Treasure carefully, 'so keep it to yourselves for a day or two. Scarbuck's company is in trouble financially. Worse than that, a rescue operation to save it from liquidation is going to disclose that Scarbuck transferred half a million pounds from Scarbuck Construction into a private company he owns himself called Forward Britain Enterprises. That's the company he used to buy Mitchell Hall from Arthur. If Scarbuck could have announced by Tuesday that he owned the holograph, any

bank would have lent him the half million to repay the loan
to Scarbuck Construction against the security of the manuscript. Without such collateral he was sunk. His creditors
are putting a receiver in mid-week.'

'But, Mark, didn't you say that the Forward Britain
Movement had plenty of money?' enquired Moonlight.

'Yes, the Movement could well afford to bail out Scarbuck,
but it's a Trust with no financial connection with Forward
Britain Enterprises. During the slanging match Scarbuck
and Speke-Jones had in front of Inspector Bantree after
Speke-Jones had confessed, it came out that a majority of
the trustees of the Movement – led by Speke-Jones – were
quite unwilling to lend Scarbuck a penny from the Movement's funds. That's partly why Scarbuck held the jamboree
here this weekend; he was hoping to persuade them dif-
ferently – especially after they'd seen the manuscript – but
it didn't work. Of course, only Speke-Jones could have
known why he desperately needed the money, but Speke-
Jones wanted Scarbuck to be disgraced publicly so that he,
Speke-Jones, could take over the Presidency of the Movement. No doubt, if this had happened with the existence of
the holograph still undisclosed, Speke-Jones would have
arranged for the Movement to take over responsibility for
the debts and assets – including the hidden one – of Enterprises, to the huge relief of any liquidator involved. In that
way Speke-Jones would have been rid of Scarbuck and
acquired the leadership of a potentially powerful and extremely rich organization. Oh yes, the man had a great deal
at stake – enough even to risk murder . . . I still think un-
premeditated, but murder nevertheless.

'How clever you are, Mark.' Elizabeth stifled a yawn.
'Now I really think we should go to bed. Thelma, why don't
you stay here for what's left of the night? – then you won't
feel obliged to join our worthy Vicar at the early service.'

Miss Goodbody agreed; then to everyone's surprise
kissed Timothy Trapp on the cheek before leaving the room
with Elizabeth.

'And what does that signify, I wonder?' Elizabeth enquired archly.

'We'll tell you tomorrow,' replied Thelma, pirouetting to
the foot of the stairs. 'We've all had enough excitement for
one day.'

Trapp said his farewells and left the study ahead of the
two older men.

'Close the door a minute, Mark, there's a good chap.'

Treasure had been making his own way to bed but he did
as he was asked. He settled into a chair opposite Moonlight.

'There was a significant and tactful lack of enquiry about
my motive for blowing a hole in the Acropolis.'

'Your first explanation is good enough for me, Arthur.'

'Yes, but I'd rather you knew the whole truth; then it
will be up to you to pass it on to the police if you see fit.'
Moonlight's tone was matter-of-fact. 'You see, in a strict
sense, I'm responsible for this whole damned mess and I'm
ready to take the consequences.'

Treasure smiled. 'You mean you planted that letter for
Dankton to find?'

Moonlight was genuinely astonished. 'How did you know?'

'After reading that report on the Diaries it seemed fairly
likely that the letter had ended up here with Sarah Moonlight
and not in some Northamptonshire hole in the wall.'

'You're quite right. I found it here along with the Diaries.
Sarah was a cool customer by all accounts but she did have
a streak of sentiment – she preserved that last contact with
her dead husband . . . Mark, six months ago I was desperate
about selling the Hall. I'm a good deal older than Elizabeth,
as you know, and the way things were it looked as though,
when I kicked the bucket, I'd be leaving her with nothing
except a white elephant and a pile of debts. Dankton came to
see me here when he discovered those other diary scraps.
Incidentally, he came with an introduction from Freddy
Canwath-Wright, I gathered they were pretty thick . . .'

'Which accounts for Dankton's actor friend knowing
the boat-house and the way to it; the chap stayed with
"Stacey" Dankton all through last summer.'

Moonlight nodded. 'Dankton invited me up to Northampton to look over this Corble Manor place – miserable pile, no wonder they were knocking it down. Anyway, on a whim, or a hunch, or whatever you want to call it I – as you said – planted the letter. It looked genuine enough; dammit, it was genuine. I don't know what I thought it would lead to. Dankton was shoving out articles on Corble by the yard. I suppose I thought that if he did one on the letter it might wake up the market a bit for the Hall. To be honest, when Scarbuck turned up with his cheque I didn't connect him with Dankton at all. Then when they arrived together two weeks ago it all fell into place. Dankton had found the letter all right, but instead of advertising it he'd used it.'

Moonlight rose and poked the dying ashes of the wood fire. Then he turned to face Treasure again. 'I knew at the time I should have come clean, spilled the beans – but I didn't and for the basest of all motives . . . money. I wanted to see the sale through to the irrevocable stage. Mark, it's difficult to live with a lie. I'd been going through hell for two weeks telling myself that the Hall was worth two hundred thousand anyway, and that Scarbuck was getting his money's worth without any holograph. Deep down though I knew he was being swindled – and swindled by me . . .'

'Very indirectly,' put in Treasure, 'and remember, he was planning to swindle you out of a great deal more than two hundred thousand.'

'In a way that's true, but two wrongs don't make a right. Then Maggie Edwards dropped dead in the churchyard. It wasn't difficult to figure how that happened. The expression on her face will haunt me for ever – I'm certain that one of those little Filipinos frightened her to death looking through the grille in the tomb.'

'That's only supposition, Arthur.'

'Yes, but it's one I gather you arrived at yourself without any help from me. Anyway, Maggie's death did it for me. I couldn't live with the lie any longer. I should have told Scarbuck the truth there and then, but curiously that seemed the coward's way out. I felt I had to pay for my dishonesty –

buy back the Hall, and get Scarbuck out of my sight.'

'There were easier ways . . .'

'I know, Mark, but they would none of them have atoned for Maggie, nor necessarily have sent Scarbuck packing.' Moonlight paused. 'But they would have saved Worple's life, and it's no thanks to me that Dankton's still alive . . . I got the idea of blowing a hole in the Acropolis some days ago. I love that little building, Mark – hurting it was like hurting myself, but it seemed a more fitting way of showing Scarbuck the place was empty than taking him by his fat little hand through the crypt. Late as it was, I thought that with you still here and the gaff blown on the treasure story, Scarbuck might see his way to selling back the Hall straight away . . . Well, that's the story Mark, and it doesn't sound very pretty, does it?'

'Not particularly,' said Treasure seriously, 'but there's a lot you haven't taken into account. Sure, I knew about Maggie Edwards, which is why I asked the local doctor about her tonight – he was here for some time after they took Dankton away. He told me categorically he'd been treating Miss Edwards for a terminal heart complaint for well over a year. Arthur, she was living on borrowed time. It's just as likely she died from over-exertion as from a fright. As for the tragedy of Worple's death, that would have happened with or without the opening up of the gallery. I've seen the place, man. The well area had never caved in, and it had never been filled in. Worple was digging a grave over a ten-foot open drop into a ruddy great well-hole. If the Filipinos hadn't used the hole for rubble – and it may have been filled in three hundred years ago for all we know – but if it hadn't been full of rocks, then Worple would certainly have broken his neck falling down the well. Remember, it was the fall that killed him, not the blades on the machine.'

'You really think so, Mark?' Moonlight clearly wanted to be convinced.

'I don't just think so – I know so. The police autopsy proved it. And don't tell me you hold yourself responsible for Speke-Jones's attack on Dankton? That little episode is far too distant along the chain of events for you to give it a second thought. Anyway, the chap's recovering fast; he should be right as rain by the time of his trial for complicity in getting rid of Worple's body and whatever else he's done – and that goes for his American friend as well.' Treasure snorted. 'I'll take a personal pleasure in hearing that chap's sentence . . . Got to hand it to him in a way, I suppose,' he added reluctantly, 'with two identities he'd have been damned difficult to link in with this affair.'

Moonlight was hardly listening to these last ruminations. 'I hope you're right about it all, Mark. Anyway, you've made me feel a whole lot better. I may be poor, but I'd like to feel I was still fairly honest . . . Who the hell can that be?' He glanced at the ringing telephone.

Treasure looked at his watch. 'I think it's my lovely young wife. She never can work out the time difference between here and the States,' he added, picking up the 'phone. 'Hello . . . yes, this is Mark Treasure . . . Hello, darling . . . yes, of course I'm all right, you're ringing me remember? . . .'

It was not until some weeks later that Arthur Moonlight, having followed Treasure's advice and come to terms with his conscience, enjoyed the bonus of discovering that he was, after all, relatively rich. Not only was Trapp's picture proved to be a Vandyck; it was also an exceptionally good one, executed – so the experts divined – by the Master himself, without the aid of pupils. Sarah Moonlight's unusually beautiful features were taken to account for the artist's personal dedication to the task of recording them in oils; they also went some way to explain the lady's almost life-long attraction for the opposite sex.

The cleaned picture fetched £240,000 at Sotheby's – an all-time record price at auction for work by this artist. Moonlight insisted on Trapp appropriating £20,000 for good works, expecting to use what was left after tax to help re-purchase Mitchell Hall, albeit against the advice of Mark Treasure.

In the event, the liquidators of Forward Britain were only too pleased to accept £100,000 for the property. Having reacquired the place, Moonlight was facing the dilemma of what to do with it when he was approached by the Committee members of the Mid-Stoke Golf Club. Tired of being bombarded by golf-balls on the terrace of their unattractive Club House, these worthies recognized the several benefits – practical, social, and aesthetic – that would accrue if they moved base to a seventeenth-century mansion complete – or nearly so – with a capacious swimming pool and room in plenty for tennis courts and a much improved putting green.

The members bought Mitchell Hall, showing a profit for Moonlight and for themselves since the old Club House was converted into expensive flats. Mid-Stoke thereafter acquired a new status in the golfing world which justified a considerable increase in membership fees. Thus the transaction was highly satisfactory for all concerned.

It will never be known how the Vandyck came to be preserved in the first place. Bishop Wringle definitely recalled the over-painted picture being relegated to the vicarage cellar by his discerning father when appointed incumbent of Mitchell Stoke. He claimed some recollection of a reported conversation between his mother and Mrs Symington concerning the earlier removal of the then whitened picture from the church, where it had done service as a draught screen – but he was not sure of the details. If some Puritan abominater of high-class harlotry had, in a frenzy of zeal, obliterated Sarah's image during the Commonwealth period, then he had inadvertently done a service for posterity. The substance he had employed for the task had proved to be an ideal preservative, as the restorers had attested.

Following the public disgrace of Arthur Scarbuck and Griffith Speke-Jones, the Forward Britain Movement was formally disbanded shortly after it informally disintegrated. Without the catalyzing influence of its two leading members, the disparity of views and aims harboured by the inharmonious groups comprising its membership soon led to bitter internal dissent. The issue was resolved and the Movement extinguished with the return of everyone's subscription. Surprisingly, all were reimbursed in full.

Thelma Goodbody and Timothy Trapp were married shortly after Whitsun – Bishop Wringle officiating, with Bach in attendance. Thelma never did acquire her doctorate, though she was able to continue her researches digging for information, physically and metaphorically, all around the parish. Her belief that Shakespeare and the King's Men had performed *As You Like It* at Mitchell Stoke was, of course, fanned into conviction by the contents of the James Moonlight letter. On the advice of her doctor, she was obliged to desist from excavating in the churchyard shortly before her first child was born in the following February. The infant, a boy, was naturally christened Oliver Jaques Orlando Trapp.